RESURGENCE

THE FOUR STAGES OF MARKET-FOCUSED REINVENTION

GREGORY S. CARPENTER, GARY F. GEBHARDT, AND JOHN F. SHERRY, JR.

St. Martin's Press
New York

www.stmartins.com

Designed by Letra Libre

Library of Congress Cataloging-in-Publication Data

Carpenter, Gregory S.
    Resurgence: the four stages of market-focused reinvention / Gregory S. Carpenter, Gary F. Gebhardt, John F. Sherry, Jr.
        p.   cm.
    ISBN 978-1-137-27861-6 (hardcover)
    1. Brand name products. 2. Branding (Marketing) 3. Entrepreneurship.
I. Gebhardt, Gary F. II. Sherry, John F., Jr. III. Title.
    HD69.B7C367   2014
    658.8'27—dc23

                                                                    2013025371

Our books may be purchased in bulk for promotional, educational, or business use. Please contact your local bookseller or the Macmillan Corporate and Premium Sales Department at 1-800-221-7945, extension 5442, or by e-mail at MacmillanSpecialMarkets@macmillan.com.

First published by Palgrave Macmillan, a division of St. Martin's Press LLC

First Edition: February 2014

10   9   8   7   6   5   4   3

CONTENTS

1
THE BEGINNING

EVERYONE KNOWS WHAT IT IS LIKE TO BE ADRIFT. ALL businesses go through it at some point, even the übersuccessful ones. Companies like Motorola, which had been a longtime leader in wireless technology until it lost its prime position in 1998 to Nokia; like Harley-Davidson, whose market share dropped into the single digits in the early 1980s under pressure from Japanese manufacturers like Honda and Suzuki; or like McDonald's, the iconic fast-food brand under pressure in the 2000s from the rise of fast-healthy options from competitors like Subway.

Such challenges are hardly unique. More than half the companies feted in *BusinessWeek* or *Forbes* cover stories will be, ten years on, struggling or also-rans. *Most,* if not all, successful companies will at some point find themselves attacked by competitors, or slow to adapt to customer change or technological shifts. Flagship products slowly lose market share and disappear. Channel partners consolidate or shift focus and leave you out. Customers, once loyal, no longer seem to want what you have.

When you're adrift and you know it, it can be hard to see the way out. Your best ideas seem to go nowhere. But further decline is not inevitable. We know—for more than ten years we have been talking to struggling companies to understand what causes them to stagnate and what allows them to break out of it. We found that companies *can* orchestrate their own turnaround. They can recapture the spark that fueled their rise, return to growth, and even eclipse their former successes. How? They need to reinvent themselves.

YOU CAN'T UNBAKE A CAKE

Leaders of stagnating businesses are often inundated with advice on how to turn things around. They are encouraged to bring in new faces; hire consultants; beef up, cut, or rejigger incentives; listen to the customer; change the culture; reorganize. Yet a recent study by IBM shows that as few as 8 percent of change efforts produce the desired results.[1] Those odds imply that companies that fail to change are doing something wrong, but the reality is much more subtle. In fact, our work shows that *the firms that remain stuck take many of the same actions as those that revitalize.* What makes the difference?

Change fails when leaders approach the process as if they were tossing a salad—chop some lettuce, dice tomatoes and cucumber, drizzle a little dressing, combine. Most change and leadership advice assumes that the *sequence* of steps does not matter. Yet we see the opposite. Change is chemical. It is more like baking a cake than salad making. The ingredients themselves may be well-known, but you need to combine the butter, sugar, eggs, flour, and heat in a particular order and with a particular technique if you want delicious results. Choosing the wrong sequence renders the ingredients useless—you can't unbake a cake.

Reinvention works according to the same principle. We've seen that when struggling businesses take specific actions *in a specific order,* they are able to return to growth, even to eclipse their past success. Put the right actions in the wrong order and companies find that the time, money, goodwill, and effort bring disappointment and dim hopes for a successful resurgence.

Through detailed case studies of seven companies we examined in depth over many years, as well as numerous other examples, we'll show you the actions—*and the sequence*—that allow firms to successfully reinvent themselves. Our work reveals how businesses like Alberto-Culver, Harley-Davidson, and Marshfield DoorSystems achieved a remarkable market-focused resurgence after finding themselves stagnant and moribund. We also identify the errors and pitfalls that have caused companies like Avon and JCPenney to circle the drain of change without ever pulling through. Experiences on both sides offer a guide for companies looking to restart a drifting company and reignite growth.

IGNITING GROWTH: THE FOUR STAGES OF MARKET-FOCUSED REINVENTION

The seven businesses we followed in depth were all, at one time, successful growth businesses whose strategies were challenged by pressure from changing markets, new competitors, or a shift in customer demand. Over time, each realized that it had lost touch with its customers and its markets. In an effort to turn the companies back toward a growth path, they all realized they needed to change.

The companies we spent time with all initiated a wholesale change effort, but not all of them were successful at revitalizing their firms. The four companies that ignited growth were distinguished by the fact that they each progressed through a four-stage path of market-focused reinvention (see Figure 1–1).

In the first stage of change—the Recognize stage—an individual or a small group of senior leaders in each organization recognizes the need for change and builds a coalition to reinvent

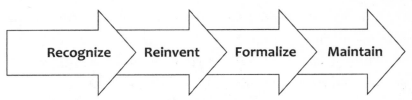

Figure 1-1:   Four Stages of a Market-Focused Reinvention

the firm. What will that change look like? How will they do it? Where will they start? The change leaders don't know the answers to these questions at this stage of the process, and the smart ones do not pretend they do. What they do know is that they have lost touch with their customers. They don't know anymore what the market wants and what they have to do to deliver it.

Recognition is the first stage of any change effort. It is also, in many cases, the most difficult. It is not uncommon for leaders of once-successful companies to ignore or underestimate the factors that are setting the business adrift. Recognition requires leaders to accept that change is needed and that those changes may upend the very systems that put them into power in the first place. It is scary, but necessary, for leaders to accept their ignorance of what the change will be. Too many leaders jump in too early in an effort to just *do* something, and more often than not they do more damage. The leaders who realized change trusted that the process of reconnecting with their customers would reveal the necessary actions for change.

In the second stage of change, known as Reinvent, the change coalition starts to put some specifics into a market-focused vision for change. Once that vision is established, the leaders take that vision public to build support within the organization. They generate the enthusiasm and encourage a set of cultural behaviors needed inside the firm to realize the vision. They then work to reconnect with the market to gain an accurate, consistent, and company-wide understanding of the market, and bring that understanding back to the firm and use it to guide improvement and strategy efforts. Reinvention is the core of the change process, and, as you will see, we spend around half the book walking you through the necessary steps of this stage. We reveal not only a number of successful approaches taken at this stage but also how change efforts commonly lose momentum when companies fail to realize any of the necessary steps within the stage—from effective communication of the change goals to concrete connection with the customer. There is no way to achieve a market-focused resurgence if you don't strike the flint of reignition at this stage.

Companies that work through the series of steps of the Reinvention stage will feel the changes that occur. They may have returned to growth, launched new products, seen an uptick in demand, or realized positive gains in the areas that are important to them. At this point, companies may feel like they are finished— they are resurgent! But it is easy to slip back down the path of stagnation. Preventing that slip requires that companies *Formalize* the practices that enabled the reinvention. Formalize is the third stage of change. It is here that companies may choose to redefine their compensation structures, to define and publish their values, and to create formal recruitment practices to ensure new hires coming into the firm share the values and priorities of the business.

The fourth and last stage is Maintain, which focuses on sustaining the cultural and behavioral changes that allowed the firm to realize its resurgence. Companies Maintain change through ongoing connection with the market and development of personnel.

Change with a Focus on the Market

The businesses we have seen successfully engineer their resurgence all employed this four-stage sequence, but the emphasis varied depending on the specific context. Harley-Davidson, for example, was drifting along with single-digit market share, a reputation for poor quality, and a contentious history with unions. Its reinvention required the entire Harley organization to realize that its products were not universally loved by the market; if the company was to survive, it needed to change.

Motorola, on the other hand, had a long history of dominating its markets—no competitors came close until the wheels fell off in the mid-1990s. Its resurgence required a dramatic shift in its engineering-dominated culture.

For all their differences, the firms that realized a successful resurgence kept one common element constant and central: customers. Successful resurgence requires the creation of a customer- and market-focused organization. None of the businesses we studied were customer-focused before their transformation. But they each embraced a set of values that identified the customer as the purpose, the raison d'être, of the business. That market focus became part of their transformation and created a culture that emphasized real customer connections as critical to ongoing success.

THE ORIGINS

We started working on this book more than ten years ago when Gary, then a PhD student at the Kellogg School of Management at Northwestern University, was working with Greg and John, both professors of marketing at Kellogg at the time, as his dissertation advisers. In those years there were a number of seemingly parallel, but eventually intersecting, trends under way within businesses seeking an edge.

On one side was a group of companies embracing the idea of "market orientation." Market orientation, or market focus as we call it interchangeably in this book, is best viewed for our purposes as a culture in which a business and its employees focus on the customer as the purpose, the raison d'être, of the firm. Market-focused firms see serving the customer's needs as the job of every employee regardless of where they sit in the organization, and they value efforts to gather insights into that customer and bring them back in-house so that everyone has a shared understanding of whom they are serving.

As a concept, market orientation was first advanced by Adam Smith more than two centuries ago, but in the modern era its greatest advocate was the management guru Peter Drucker, whose most famous phrase on the subject dictates that the purpose of a business is to *create* a customer. More elaborately, Drucker wrote, "Marketing is not only much broader than selling, it is not a specialized activity at all. It encompasses the entire business. It is the whole business seen from the point of view of its final result, that is, from the customer's point of view. Concern and responsibility for marketing must therefore permeate all areas of the enterprise."[2]

The concept felt intuitively right to many who heard it, but Drucker didn't offer much to practitioners who needed guidance on what it actually looked like in practice to run a business from the point of view of the final result—how exactly can a company operate in a way to ensure success in that effort? And how can leaders assess when the business was falling short by that measure? Those details were left to the academics Ajay Kohli and Bernard Jaworski, who went on in 1990 to create a basic framework that gave business leaders some way to measure how market-focused their firms were.[3]

Kohli and Jaworski offered a concrete definition of what market orientation is. Others then went out to assess whether having a market orientation helps—do businesses in fact do better when they operate, as Drucker suggested, with the view of the customer at the center of what they do? The broad conclusion from the research is yes. Multiple studies have revealed that market-oriented companies have more satisfied and loyal customers than their less market-oriented competitors; they are more innovative and bring more successful new products and services to market; internally their employees are more satisfied and intrinsically motivated; they enjoy higher levels of profitability and stock market returns; and their returns are less volatile.[4]

At the same time that the market-orientation movement was gaining more traction and clarity, the corporate "change" movement was exploding. Corporate leaders across all sectors were realizing that their processes, cultures, products—almost everything about the way they operated—were ill suited to the new competitive dynamics they faced. Accelerating cross-sector and cross-geographical integration and competition required a different set of approaches and norms within their companies. The "change" movement promised these leaders a set of methods that would help them adjust to changes faster. Many popular approaches promoted the idea that effective, sustained change happens through a staged process, one legacy of which is the popularity of the Six Sigma and Lean process improvement methodologies.

Market orientation and effective change began dominating the business imagination at around the same time, but no one was considering how these trends converge. Plenty of energy had gone into figuring out how companies change to produce higher-quality products, or to be more efficient with the resources they have. But few people were asking how formerly inward-facing or silo-dominated companies change to become more market-focused. We saw an opportunity to ask the question, and we sought the answer to it by designing an in-depth study of seven companies that had gone adrift and, in response, initiated a market-focused resurgence.

THE RESEARCH AND THE COMPANIES

The original research study involved seven businesses operating in seven distinct industries. The named companies in the original study are Alberto-Culver, a consumer goods company with more than $2 billion in revenue in 2002, most famous for the Alberto VO5 line of hair care products; Harley-Davidson, the iconic motorcycle manufacturer that nearly collapsed in the early 1980s under competitive pressure from Honda, Kawasaki, and Suzuki; Marshfield DoorSystems, a door manufacturer with $125 million in revenue in 2001, owned by the corporate giant Weyerhaeuser; and Motorola PCS, the $10 billion arm of the famed equipment manufacturer (PCS is responsible for personal communications devices such as mobile phones and pagers).

Three other companies agreed to participate anonymously, including BenefitsInc, a $10 billion benefits management company formed through the merger of two smaller organizations; EquipmentCo, an industrial equipment manufacturer owned by a $3 billion corporate parent we refer to as HoldingsInc; and MediaCo, a respected $2 billion media services firm.

When we started this research in 2001, each of these companies was in one of the four stages of a market-focused resurgence. MediaCo, BenefitsInc, and EquipmentCo, for instance, were just beginning their change efforts and had barely entered the Reinvent stage. Motorola was somewhat more advanced, having progressed through to the end of the Reinvent stage. Alberto-Culver and Marshfield DoorSystems were in the process of Formalizing change. Harley-Davidson, for its part, had gone through its intense reinvention stage in the 1980s and 1990s and was focusing, at the time of the fieldwork, on maintaining that momentum (see Figure 1–2).

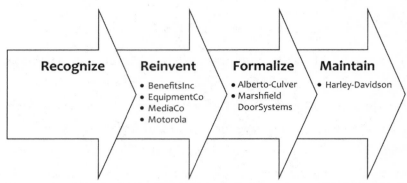

Figure 1-2:   The Study Participants Were at Different Stages When We Began Our Research

Gary spent time on-site at each of these firms. Over the course of ten months he conducted more than seventy qualitative interviews with employees and leaders and amassed a total of 120 hours of interview materials. The goal of these interviews was to get an understanding of the change the informants had experienced and the steps they took. Gary conducted the interviews using an ethnographic approach, in which he structured the interviews to operate more as conversations and oral histories. His questions were open-ended and he let the subjects guide the emphasis, though we worked as a team to adjust the questions themselves over time to test our theories and to capture changes and adjustments as they were happening.

In addition to the qualitative interviews, Gary was also "embedded" within these organizations in a way that gave him a firsthand feel for the changes that were under way—he did not need to rely solely on the memories of his interviewees. He attended meetings, was invited to events, sat in the lunchroom, and engaged with employees. He was also given access by many of these companies to artifacts and historical documents from the change effort. These included in-house planning documents or documentation, video or audio, and other concrete sources that allowed us to verify and deepen the analysis of the interviews.

From those sources we identified the four stages of a market-focused reinvention, but we did not stop there. Instead, we brought our findings to the businesses and leaders whom we teach and advise in our roles as business school academics. These interactions have allowed us to identify other companies that went through similar experiences and confirm that those companies that successfully realize a market-focused resurgence follow a shockingly similar path, despite their different industries and histories. Likewise, companies whose change efforts flame out make most of the same mistakes.

THE BOOK

This book moves progressively through the four stages of a market-focused resurgence as seen through the stories of the seven companies Gary spent time with doing field research. As the stories of these businesses unfold, we show the incremental steps needed to Recognize, Reinvent, Formalize, and Maintain change (see Figure 1–3). We also highlight the mistakes these companies made

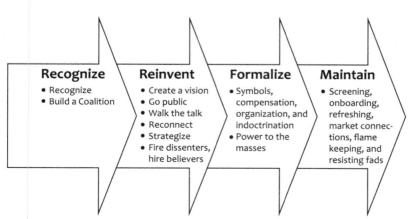

Figure 1-3:   Each Stage Involves Incremental Steps

in an attempt to turn around a flagging firm. Whenever it makes sense, we supplement these core stories with examples we have uncovered of other companies working to realize market-focused change—companies like Avon, JCPenney, eBay, McDonald's, and Starbucks.

All direct quotes, unless otherwise noted in the endnotes, came from firsthand interviews that Gary conducted while he was doing field research. We never name the speaker of quotes from our primary research—we chose to take this approach in order to encourage the informant to be open, and to maintain the privacy of the source.[5] We do strive to give context to the comments by identifying an informant's title or position in the business. We have assigned pseudonyms to refer to the executives at BenefitsInc, MediaCo, and EquipmentCo.

LESSONS FOR ALL

All businesses, young or old, large or small, need to learn how to ignite growth, since every company in every industry will at some point find itself adrift. The lessons of resurgence apply likewise not just to companies but to divisions, departments, and even in some cases individual managers. So let's get started. In the next chapter we introduce our companies as they Recognize the need for change.

2

MY NAME IS MOTOROLA AND I HAVE A PROBLEM

Recognizing the Need for Change

MOTOROLA'S PERSONAL COMMUNICATIONS SECTOR (PCS) business was remarkably successful before it began to cede ground in the mobile phone era. Established in 1928, Motorola was founded to manufacture technology that lets radios operate without a battery. The company later developed a number of major innovations in radio technology, which allowed it to forge lucrative relationships with the US military and NASA and to play important roles in world events. For example, Motorola radios and the invention of the walkie-talkie enabled Allied troops to more effectively coordinate actions during World War II. Motorola's success reached otherworldly heights when its technology transmitted Neil Armstrong's famous line, "That's one small step for man, one giant leap for mankind," from the moon. Back on earth, Motorola engineer Martin Cooper placed the very first cellular phone call using a Motorola device, starting a mobile communications revolution that has reached more than one billion consumers.

The focus on pioneering technology allowed Motorola to enjoy 80 percent market share in nearly every product category it sold. Motorola also took pride in having world-class processes— the company that turned Six Sigma into a brand in its own right knew something about quality management.

Motorola's history of remarkable, unchallenged success created a culture that celebrated engineering prowess above all else. Engineering reigned for decades, elevated to the extent that engineering-centric behaviors calcified into hardwired survival behavior—anyone who wanted to advance in the organization did so by either working as an engineer or supporting engineering. Such hero worship made sense as long as the company's proven skill at creating new, innovative technologies went unmatched, as it did for decades. People who worked in engineering saw themselves, and were seen, as the lifeblood of the firm, its celebrated heart and soul. People who worked in other departments—particularly marketing—were dismissed as "failed engineers."

A history of extreme success, and the cultural behaviors it produced, made recognizing the full gravity of the challenges ahead very difficult for Motorola. When the lauded PCS division, which designed, manufactured, sold, and serviced a variety of mobile end-user devices, began losing market share in the early 1990s to other mobile device manufacturers, the PCS leaders essentially ignored it. A high-profile executive asserted that the division had a "God-given right to 80 percent market share," even as Motorola PCS struggled to compete against rising rivals. For more than five years, the view of the "God-given right" prevailed. Motorola PCS products had to fall to the number-two spot behind Nokia in 1998 before the leaders were willing to stand up and recognize their potential vulnerability.

Fortunately, becoming number two cut right at the core of Motorola culture. Number two might be great for someone else—Samsung, say, or Sony. But Motorola had *invented* cellular technology. It had been the leader in radio communication and expected that success to continue with cellular. No one else had ever before come close. Only an event that served as an affront to its identity could have broken through the denial that had paralyzed the firm and made it unable to change.

"This is kind of like Alcoholics Anonymous," said one Motorola executive who was part of Motorola's eventual resurgence. "You step up to the mic and you recognize that you have a problem. And I think for us, we had to recognize that we had a problem around the fact that we weren't market-oriented and it was manifesting itself in the fact that we were delivering products that our customers weren't really clamoring for—or that the consumers weren't really jumping to buy."

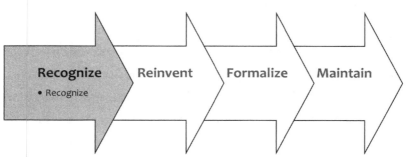

Figure 2-1:   The First Step of Stage One: Recognize

RECOGNITION: WHEN YOUR
COMPANY NEEDS AN INTERVENTION

To Recognize the need for change is both the first stage of change, and the first step in the change process (see Figure 2-1). Recognition is an essential part of the process, yet it is often the most difficult stage to realize. This is especially true for companies like Motorola, whose great success had instilled a set of cultural norms and practices that slow, complicate, or even prevent change.

Past success—whether nominal or extreme—acts in every struggling company to create and reinforce the culture and norms of behavior that existed during that successful era. The lesson that so many companies learn is that they are successful *because* of both what they do and the way they do it. Motorola, for example, tied its success to an aggressive, engineering-focused culture that dismissed the contributions of other departments; Alberto-Culver to the creativity and salesmanship of its founder, Leonard Lavin; iconic Harley-Davidson to a combination of engineering and a history of creating products that police forces, the US military, and American riders would always buy.

These cultural qualities can be very important to many companies. They can also be limiting. When the market changes, or a creative leader steps down, the company is left with a set of norms and behaviors that not only fail to serve the market but can also be a liability. They are lessons of the past that do little to prepare the firm for the present.

Recognizing that the company's established culture and values are ill suited for what lies ahead is difficult on an emotional level. Executives with companies that have been extremely successful in the past may ignore the warning signs out of a deep sense of denial. Even if you've not been part of the kind of market leadership seen at Motorola, it can be hard to admit that a strategy you imagined, promoted, and invested in has not produced the results you promised. When the Motorola executive quoted above likened his company's experience of recognition to an alcoholic admitting her alcoholism, it was an apt comparison. Recognition often has to challenge fundamental beliefs and cut through plenty of atavistic optimism, deep-seated denial, ambivalence, and counterarguments before it rises to the surface.

Recognition is the difficult act of seeing that your company is facing challenges that it is not equipped to meet. Recognition includes admitting that a challenge is real—not a fad or a temporary lull, but a real, definitive threat to the company's survival. And it includes admitting that the company is vulnerable, that it does not have what it needs at that moment to tackle the challenge. Perhaps it does not have a product that can meet a new market need; perhaps it does not have the financial or human resources to walk the obvious path to meet a challenge. Most often, it does not have the culture or organization or people necessary to confront the challenge.

As Motorola's story makes clear, company history and culture can play a huge role in how quickly leaders recognize the need for change. Motorola sustained five years of falling market share without any meaningful reaction. Denial was a strong cause of inertia in that case, but denial is not unique to the übersuccessful. Companies that do solid business in the middle of their markets can also ignore clear warning signs. Fear, ambivalence, routine, poor morale, or lack of motivation—any of these factors (and all companies have at least one) can prevent leaders from recognizing true threats.

WARNING SIGNS: WHEN THE MARKET SIGNALS A NEED FOR CHANGE

Poor or unanticipated financial results offer companies the clearest sign of a need for change. It certainly sent very clear signs to

Harley-Davidson.[1] The iconic motorcycle manufacturer was already a legend by the early 1980s. Founded in 1903, it built its reputation in its early years as a trusted provider of motorcycle fleets for law enforcement and the military. Harley-Davidson made its first sale to a police department in 1908. Later, it supplied the US military with twenty thousand motorcycles, which couriers and messengers used during World War I to carry messages between leaders at the front. (This is an ironic coincidence given that Motorola's technology had replaced hand delivery by the time World War II began. Harley-Davidson did fine anyway, delivering even more vehicles for the World War II effort.)

Such lucrative government relationships allowed Harley-Davidson to hang on through the competitive turmoil of the first half of the twentieth century, including the Great Depression. During that time, dozens of motorcycle manufacturers tried, and failed, to dominate the US market, but by the 1950s Harley-Davidson was one of the country's only surviving motorcycle manufacturers. More striking, in 1959, Harley-Davidson enjoyed over 80 percent market share, with its nearest rival in single digits.[2]

That position came under threat just a few years later, in the 1960s, when Honda and Suzuki entered the North American market with superior products. The Japanese rivals built factories in the United States, and Honda, initially ignored by Harley-Davidson, overtook the American icon on its own turf in just a few short years. Suzuki, Kawasaki, and other competitors also saw their respective sales grow exponentially, and by the 1970s Harley was in serious financial trouble. The company survived that decade as a wholly owned subsidiary of American Machine and Foundry Corporation (AMF), but the parent did nothing to change or reinvent Harley, and by 1981 the motorcycle manufacturer was again independent and barely holding on—with only 5 percent market share. Finally, its leadership team initiated change.

Financial pressures also provided the leading signal for Marshfield DoorSystems. The custom door manufacturer, a subsidiary of Weyerhaeuser, had experienced multimillion-dollar losses for a number of years when the Weyerhaeuser executive in charge of doors decided to take action.

COMPANIES	FINANCIAL PRESSURE	MARKET DISRUPTION	UNCOMPETITIVE PRODUCTS	LOST MARKET POSITION	LOW MORALE
Alberto-Culver		O			O
BenefitsInc	O				O
EquipmentCo	O		O		O
Harley-Davidson	O		O	O	O
Marshfield DoorSystems	O		O		O
MediaCo		O			O
Motorola	O		O	O	O

Figure 2-2:   Challenges that Ignite Recognition

Change Is Inevitable

In a way, Harley-Davidson and Marshfield DoorSystems were lucky. Not all firms have the benefit of a clear and obvious sign, like financial woes, to signal the need for change (see Figure 2-2). Alberto-Culver, for example, had been riding the wave of a banner year in 1992, with more than $1 billion in sales and record profits. But there were rumblings of concern underneath the triumph: Walmart had taken the crown as the top retailer in the United States, and consolidation among Alberto-Culver distributors was rampant, creating fierce competition in the consumer packaged-goods industry. These trends were leading to lower margins on flagship products, such as VO5 and TRESemmé. Internally, employee morale was at an all-time low, resulting in high rates of turnover.

The media company we refer to as MediaCo was likewise an industry leader in 2001 when its leaders began to recognize that the advertising business would be threatened by the growth of the Internet. The terrorist attacks of September 11, 2001, then caused a real drop in advertising that only accelerated the inevitable industry change.

The range illustrated by these examples makes clear that the signs can vary dramatically. Some companies can be near bankruptcy before the need for change is apparent. Others see the signs on the horizon in the forms of industry disruptions, new competition from nontraditional players, or even new regulation.

Some companies may receive signals based on the status of others in their market. The online auction pioneer eBay, for example, was doing well by many measures in the early 2000s. The users of its auction site had expanded beyond the collectors and enthusiasts who brought it initial fame. But in the fast-growth culture of Silicon Valley, companies like Amazon and Apple were doing spectacularly well and eBay was, comparatively, just doing okay. The negative comparison made clear to the leadership that eBay needed to reignite growth. Without the change, the auction platform was destined to be squeezed between the consumer embrace of online retailers like Amazon—with its expanding range of products and innovative fulfillment system—and the online presence of traditional retailers.

The inevitable nature of disruption makes the case for a market-focused reinvention. Whether the business is a market leader fallen on hard times, or a mid-market player facing market disruptions, those that have put in place a culture that is focused on the customer and are in touch with the needs and the changes happening on the customer level will maintain—even exceed—their past success.

THE ROLE OF LEADERS:
RESURGENCE AS AN ELITIST REVOLUTION

Carol Bernick was the newly appointed president of Alberto-Culver's North America operation when she recognized that the company her parents had founded forty years before was going to be in for some difficult years.

Leonard and Bernice Lavin founded Alberto-Culver in 1955. Leonard Lavin was an independent entrepreneur at the time. Though he had his home base in Chicago, he made his living as a traveling salesman for a number of different manufacturers. While in Los Angeles one day he reportedly saw a display for Alberto VO5 conditioning treatment. The product was marketed for its ability to protect the hair of movie actors under hot stage lights. Lavin bought the Alberto VO5 business outright and began traveling around the country selling it to pharmacies and other retail stores. From those origins, Alberto-Culver grew from a family-run business into an international, multimillion-dollar manufacturer of hair and skin care products.[3]

By the time Bernick occupied the president's chair she had a long history with the company her parents founded. That history and corporate loyalty might have predisposed her toward denial. But she also had a very clear message sent to her early in her tenure that she wouldn't ignore. Namely, in 1992 the head of human resources for Alberto-Culver contracted with a consulting company to conduct an employee satisfaction survey, which the HR executive wanted to use as part of an effort to revise the company's compensation policy. The consulting firm recommended they conduct the survey by randomly sampling the employee base, but

Bernick suggested instead that it survey only the top one hundred performers—Mr. and Mrs. Lavin were still the CEO and head of operations at the time, and Bernick believed her parents would trust the opinions only of those employees they valued most.

But the consultant's advice prevailed. As Bernick explained, "To get the best of both worlds, the consultant surveyed that group as well as a more general employee group and reported the results in tandem. The satisfaction levels of the two groups differed, of course. But the eye-opener was that neither was very satisfied. Even our best people complained about noncompetitive benefits, opaque policies, and lack of family-friendly policies, to name just a few."[4]

At the time, Alberto-Culver's extremely high rate of employee turnover was widely known. The survey gave Bernick some clarity about why people tended to work for the company for a short time and then leave. The possibility that her best talent might continue to leave under her leadership provided a real wake-up call for Carol Bernick. She was in the process of transitioning into one of the top leadership roles, and was given a clear message about the level of low morale and turnover within the most productive ranks of the company. She had no idea what change would bring, of course, but she knew that she needed to initiate a change effort if she was going to have the knowledge, talent, and cohesion needed to lead the company through the retail sector disruptions and shrinking margins that were threatening the business. She never said this outright, but change was a matter of survival.

While the exact details of the situation vary depending on the company, we have consistently seen that the recognition of the need for change has to happen at the highest levels. Marshfield DoorSystems benefited from the insight of a corporate executive from Weyerhaeuser, the firm's corporate parent, who saw the losses in its subsidiary and realized he would need to act.

Harley-Davidson's change efforts were led by one of its thirteen owner/investors, Vaughn Beals. The need for change at Motorola was evangelized by a group of senior executives, including Robert Galvin, former chairman and son of the founder, and Chris Galvin, grandson of the founder and the firm's COO since 1993. A subset of senior executives saw the need to transform BenefitsInc, and the chairman and CEO of MediaCo initiated that firm's change. We could go on, but you get the point—recognition needs to happen at the top.

There is a conflict inherent in requiring that leaders spearhead change, since those same leaders have a vested interest in keeping things as they are. Change, after all, is dynamic and uncertain. Leaders can't really control it, and they cannot be sure, once initiated, how the change effort will affect them personally. For most, the certainty of the status quo is far superior to the risks of change—that is the reason most resistance movements and revolutions start with a group of disadvantaged people fighting for change. Revolutionaries are most often those without power.

In struggling businesses, however, the revolution starts at the top. The people in power need to see that the institution is broken and they need to be willing to stand up to opposing factions (board members, competing executives, etc.) to launch a revolution within the firm. We have not seen any examples of successful market-focused reinvention initiated in the grass roots of the company.

Leadership Tenure and Successful Change

Interestingly, recognition seems to happen more often in firms with new leaders. Carol Bernick had been with Alberto-Culver most of her career, but she had only just been promoted as the North American president when she recognized the need for change and initiated the effort. Her story about the human resources survey, and her instinct to limit it to only the top-hundred performers based on her parents' attitudes about whose views mattered, says a great deal about the type of organization she took over and the leadership style of her predecessors. Long-tenured leaders who trust the voice and perspective of only a small percentage of the workforce are not likely to hear the rumbles of change even if they are loud and unmistakable. Alberto-Culver needed someone new, with a fresh perspective, to see the problem as it was and act on it.

Likewise, Arnold Curtis of Weyerhaeuser had only recently taken over as the vice president in charge of Marshfield Door-Systems when he tapped Bill Blankenship, another Weyerhaeuser executive, to make changes at the door maker. MediaCo's CEO Bob Smith had been leading the company for only two or three years when he began a quiet, and sadly truncated, quest for change. The chairman and CEO of the manufacturing firm EquipmentCo joined the firm in 1990 and began building his coalition in preparation for change efforts that became apparent to the broader firm four years later.

Change can of course be led by leaders with a long tenure in the executive suite, but in our experience change happens *faster* in firms with a new or newish executive. The speed of change increases when executives come into their jobs with a market-focused point of view matched by a personal value system that includes genuine respect for the firm's employees. Curtis, Bernick, Blankenship—all these people were deeply knowledgeable about the organizations they were tasked with leading, but their status at the helm was new.

This finding cuts against much of what we see in the change literature. Some persuasively argue that leaders can be taught to change. We by no means intend to discourage companies from investing in employee development, especially for highly valued executives. But our research and experiences show that long-tenured leaders have real difficulty making the transition. Even when they successfully make the change, doing so takes longer. The speed and success of change in companies that we studied were *inversely proportional* to the leadership tenure of the change leader and the members of his or her coalition.

There is an important caveat about the ability of new leaders to make change, however. In short, the leader may be new, but he or she cannot be just passing through—the individual has to be in it for the long haul. One Alberto-Culver executive described the ideal change leader when he said, "It is the leader or the change agent that makes it happen and there are three things that leader has to be. Number one, sincere. You can't just say you want something to happen, but not live it, breathe it, and have the courage to stick with it. The second thing is credibility. As in the case of any organization, the organization's not going to move in the direction the leader wants to move unless that leader has credibility. The third thing is staying power. In today's corporate world, executives change quite frequently. So you have to have staying power and the organization has to know you're going to be around for awhile. In our case, our leader, of course, was Carol Bernick. And she fits all those bills. She's one hundred percent sincere and honest and caring in all she does and her credibility is very high and being a very big stockholder, she's going to stay around. So she had all that."

The Need for Change Is Urgent, the Direction of Change Is Unclear

One of the more incredible aspects of recognition is the fact that it can be at once unambiguous and completely vague. Leaders saw the need for change as nonnegotiable. Once recognition took place, these leaders knew that their businesses were not equipped in their current incarnation to survive the challenges they faced.

Yet it would be wrong to suggest that any of them knew exactly what they needed to do, how to do it, and what the outcome would be. In fact, none of them did. But the need for change was clear. Alberto-Culver, Harley-Davidson, Marshfield DoorSystems, and MediaCo all knew that they had lost their way within their markets and with their customers. To paraphrase the Motorola executive quoted at the beginning of this chapter, these companies were making products that the customers did not want to buy.

The need for change from this early stage coalesced around a core need to become more customer- and market-focused and to reconnect with the customer in an authentic, deep way. That was as far as it went at that point. What the change would look like and the finer points of how they would pursue it were still up in the air.

An informant from Marshfield DoorSystems said that the leader charged with making change at Marshfield did not come into his role with an immediate plan for change. Instead, he was adamant that Marshfield DoorSystems needed first to understand the customers. The informant said, "We need to understand the market. Marketing 101. Go out and ask everyone involved in the chain what's important. Bring it all together."

CONCLUSION

Resurgence begins first when top executives recognize that the company has lost its way with the customer. In this revolution of elites, an individual or group of individuals with the greatest amount of power must acknowledge that the strategies they blessed—perhaps even invented—are not working.

Far from being unique to the seven companies in our original study, this need to recognize change and the nature of the leader in the best position to do it is consistent: Lou Gerstner initiated change at IBM as a new CEO and his effort led to an explosion in profit in the 1990s; Andrea Jung, the once-feted former CEO of Avon, was promoted from COO to replace a long-tenured CEO and initiated a sadly failed effort to realize resurgence of the sleepy beauty brand; at eBay, CEO Meg Whitman had begun taking steps to move the company in a different direction during in the early 2000s, but the real engine of reinvention took off after Whitman stepped down in 2007 and the eBay board promoted John Donahoe, who'd been with the company since 2005 as president of eBay Marketplaces.

The companies we spent time with and many others have to begin here—with recognition that change is essential to survival. Once recognition has happened, companies that engineer a successful resurgence are ready to take the next step in the Recognize stage of change: building a coalition.

3

TEAMS MAKE CHANGE

Building a Coalition

BY THE LATE 1970S, AMERICAN MACHINE AND FOUNDRY (AMF) spread the word that it was ready to sell Harley-Davidson. AMF had owned the iconic motorcycle manufacturer since 1969, presiding over a rough period when Honda and Suzuki took off as the manufacturers of choice. By the end of the decade, Harley-Davidson had suffered severe losses, acquired a deserved reputation for poor quality, and had a contentious relationship with its employees' union. AMF saw no path to profitability and stopped making investments in research and development. The company languished; no established businesses expressed interest in buying it.

But a group of Harley loyalists kept the faith. In 1981, thirteen members of the Harley-Davidson management team executed a leveraged buyout (LBO). Harley's thirteen owners were very clear that as soon as the sale closed they would need to begin the process of dramatic change.

The hurdles mounted. Immediately after the LBO the United States slipped into recession, which further limited sales. Rifts had also begun to form between the new owner/managers. Two participants in the LBO got cold feet about the nature of change that was needed. It was no secret that Harley-Davidson's very survival was at stake—survival that was in no way ensured by the LBO. Within months, the two investors were replaced by Richard Teerlink, who rose to become the company's CEO from 1989 to 1997; and by Tom Gelb, who was the senior vice president of operations when he retired in 1997.

This core group of Harley-Davidson leaders formed a change coalition. Led by the change leader Vaughn Beals, the group began building support throughout the organization for a wholesale change program.

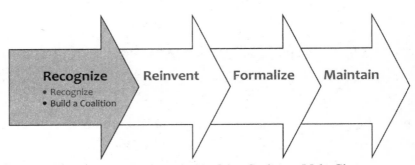

Figure 3-1:   Leaders Recognize the Need, but Coalitions Make Change

LEADERS RECOGNIZE THE NEED, BUT COALITIONS MAKE CHANGE HAPPEN

When individual leaders or groups first recognize the need for change, the impulse to *just do something* can be intense. At this early stage, change leaders are inclined to pull every possible lever—reorganize, hire people, fire people, change incentive programs, bring in Six Sigma or Lean experts to moderate an improvement initiative, reach out to customers for learning sessions, or take other incremental actions. Some of these steps may be necessary. They may even be powerful, depending on the stature of the leader. When Alberto-Culver's Carol Bernick began shifting the members of her leadership team to prepare for change, people took notice.

But too much aggressive action at this stage can be premature, especially as it pertains to major shifts like reorganizing or incentives. Leaders don't know exactly what changes they need yet, or what kind of organizational structure makes sense in light of those changes. Nor have they built the necessary support inside the organization to make change happen.

The most important action companies can take at this point is to build a team (see Figure 3-1). We admit that can be a hard effort to justify when your business is in trouble. Leaders of businesses that are losing money may be under so much pressure to stop the bleeding that they may feel pressured to take more decisive action. It is much easier and faster to hire a consultant or reorganize the business than it is to take the time to methodically staff a change team with like-minded people. But we have consistently seen that without a change coalition focused on creating a shared set of values, the actions companies take often take place too soon or too reactively, before the change leader has developed the knowledge and built the support that is necessary—even critical—for relevant and sustained change.

No one sets out to fail. But when change leaders take incremental steps without first building support and developing a shared view of the organizational change they are creating, they often lack both the necessary insights to allow for proper design and execution and the necessary support to navigate hurdles. The result is serial investments in incremental change that bring either no results, poor results, or results too siloed and circumstantial to have broad, organization-wide impact. When this happens it can erode the faith people have in the leader and his ability to make change happen. Any subsequent change effort then has to break through this organizational cynicism.

We said in the previous chapter that recognition needs to happen at the highest level. But leaders cannot execute change on their own. They need the formal support of a group of influential and like-minded individuals within the organization. In the same way that Harley-Davidson's thirteen employee/owners came together for the LBO and then worked after the deal was done to identify and operationalize change, all organizations need effective, high-ranking leaders working together if change is going to happen.

A SUCCESSFUL CHANGE COALITION

Effective change coalitions share characteristics that affect their success. At the top of the list is the fact that coalition members have a shared set of values, and the collective influence of effective coalitions reaches through to all the relevant parts of the organization.

Shared values are the foundation of an effective coalition. Resurgent companies built coalitions comprising a group of stakeholders who had a shared set of values and who agreed on the general nature of the change. More specifically, the change coalition members all recognized that their companies were in trouble; that the leaders could not effect change without the contribution of every employee in the organization; and that as a first step they needed to work to create a culturally communicative and collaborative organization.

Companies that realized their resurgence saw from the outset that these values of collaboration and communication were not part of the culture of their firms and that they needed to be. *Everyone* in the organization needed to adopt a common set of values. The way those values would translate into concrete benefits for the company was not yet clear, but the general idea held that shifting to a more collaborative culture was the key to success.

Agreement and cohesion on the need to turn to the market and have market needs guide change is likewise foundational. In the case of Harley-Davidson, the thirteen LBO investors did not all agree on the nature of the change needed. As a preparatory step, two members needed to leave in order that a coalition with a cohesive view of the firm's future could be formed.

Not every company we saw was as successful at forming a change coalition that acted with a unified set of values and a consistent perspective. Inconsistent messages and unclear direction were in fact an ongoing challenge to change at the heavy equipment manufacturer EquipmentCo. One executive from the marketing department said, "We had our leadership conference two days ago and . . . it became evident to me at this meeting that some people are standing up on the stage and saying one thing and other people are standing up on the stage and saying other things. Some people are saying, 'It's not about volume, it's about selling value. I want to find the value in our [products] and collect for that value.' And another executive will stand up and say, 'It's all about volume. We need to drive volume.' So I think that from a messaging standpoint at the very senior executive level, folks need to get on the same page."

It is important to remember that the companies that were successful in their efforts to create change did not know at this early stage of the change process exactly what the change was going to look like or what kind of outcomes it might produce. As a result, there was definitely a lack of specificity, but it stopped far short of coalition members contradicting each other. On the contrary, they were all consistent in the way they spoke about the future of the company and the need to act as a team inside the firm as part of the effort to define the direction of change outside with the market.

Part of that consistency may have resided in the fact that coalitions were not fully democratic. There was still a leader at the helm. Carol Bernick was clearly in charge at Alberto-Culver, as was Bill Blankenship at Marshfield DoorSystems and Mike Zafirovski at Motorola PCS—with the blessing of Motorola scion Chris Galvin. Harley-Davidson's thirteen-member coalition comprised many senior leaders who had long tenure with the company, but President Vaughn Beals was clearly leading the pack. A participant reflecting on that time said, "Vaughn will tell you that he tried to be as inclusive as he could, and he'd always consult the other shareholders before decisions were made. . . . But those times really demanded, I think, an autocracy, not a democracy. There was never any doubt that there were thirteen shareholders—but Vaughn was in charge."

Beyond those shared views, it matters how you organize the coalition and where it resides in the organization. Companies make one of three common organizational mistakes with their coalitions that can affect their chances for successful change. They create a coalition that is too small or too limited in its influence; they isolate coalition members in one department or function, such as marketing; or they structure the coalition too informally, so it lacks the influential authority it needs (see Table 3-1). For Harley-Davidson, Marshfield DoorSystems, and Alberto-Culver, influence over the whole organization was critical, and they achieved that influence by forming coalitions made up of members with a broad collective reach into the organization.

Successful	Coalition Characteristics	Unsuccessful
Insiders	Members	Outsiders
Shared	Values	Varied
Integrated	Structure	Isolated
Broad Cross-functional	Influence	Narrow Uni-functional
People & Culture	Focus	Siloed projects
Market understanding	Solutions	"Functional" experts

Table 3-1:   Characteristics of an Effective Coalition

KEEPING THE COALITION IN THE FAMILY

Companies vary in their approaches to building change coalitions. Organizations that *successfully* achieved a market-focused resurgence built their coalitions through an internal process of tapping known professionals from different divisions of the company. In the case of Harley-Davidson, the LBO served as a test run for the kind of cooperation and agreement that would be needed.

The effective change coalitions we saw included—were even dominated by—seasoned, invested participants, like those at Harley-Davidson. The benefit of having those kinds of participants is that they have a huge amount of credibility. In the specific case of Harley-Davidson, the men involved had just invested their own money to save the firm. They had plenty of literal and emotional capital betting on Harley-Davidson, and as a result, other stakeholders—such as the union and the employees—felt confident that their efforts were in good faith and necessary for the survival of the business.

The Coalition at Marshfield DoorSystems

There was a similar dynamic of credibility in the change coalition at Marshfield DoorSystems. Arnold Curtis, the Weyerhaeuser Group vice president in charge of Marshfield, was the first to recognize that Marshfield DoorSystems needed change to break its pattern of losses. Curtis had recently been promoted to oversee Marshfield, but he had plenty of connections within the Weyerhaeuser family, as well as a reputation for being highly focused on seeking market differentiation in the companies he led. Starting resurgence at Marshfield DoorSystems required, in his view, some respected and powerful figures at the helm.

He tapped Bill Blankenship to lead the effort. Blankenship had a reputation as a Weyerhaeuser "fixpert," an executive skilled at transforming struggling businesses. Blankenship then recruited Jerry Mannigel to work with him on the effort. Mannigel was the general manager of a Marshfield DoorSystems manufacturing plant. Blankenship and Mannigel had worked together before and shared many personal values concerning the importance of people and the need to collaborate with different departments in the organization.

Jerry Mannigel's inclusion in the change coalition sent a clear message to Marshfield DoorSystems employees. Bill Blankenship was a known quantity at Marshfield, but the fact that he lived in Seattle made his status more like that of a distant cousin than a close family member. Jerry Mannigel, on the other hand, had grown up in Marshfield, Wisconsin, and both his father and his son worked for Weyerhaeuser. Mannigel had a local-boy-done-good reputation that had been further cemented by his status as the builder and manager of one of Weyerhaeuser's most technologically advanced plants, known for strong cooperation and positive relations between the union and management. Together, Blankenship and Mannigel offered living proof of strong loyalty and commitment both to the Weyerhaeuser parent and to the people of Marshfield DoorSystems.

Once the two executives were established as cochairs of the coalition, Mannigel then worked within Marshfield DoorSystems to recruit a few more of the company's stars and further built the coalition.

Alberto-Culver's Workplace 2000

The story of credibility and loyalty in the change coalition at Alberto-Culver is very similar. In the previous chapter, which was about the need to recognize the need for change, we quoted an Alberto-Culver executive who shared his views that Carol Bernick was the ideal change leader on account of her sincerity and the personal interest she had in seeing Alberto-Culver succeed. That same executive went on to share his views on why the change coalition Bernick formed was effective.

He said, "[Besides having an effective change leader], the second success factor was to put together a core team of disciples. People that can make things happen in the organization. People that you can trust and be open and honest and not afraid of any backlash or any leakage of a thought before it's really been birthed into action. It's got to be a ripple effect. It's got to emanate the sincerity, the honesty, you can't just say the words. In our case Carol picked a small group of VPs and we were her Workplace 2000 committee, that's what we called it, and we spent years changing the culture."

The Benefits of Building Change with Known People

Building a change coalition with people known to the organization has a number of practical advantages. The coalition members already understand the company and its culture and have a better feel for the interim steps and conversations that are necessary to build support for change. There is less of a possibility that the change coalition will make dramatic mistakes in etiquette or procedure, or that they will be dismissed as outsiders whose views are irrelevant to the company.

For instance, the Workplace 2000 team that the Alberto-Culver executive refers to was formed through the promotion and parallel repositioning of people Carol Bernick had worked with before and whose ideas about market focus were consistent with where she believed the company needed to go. A number of informants reported that by the time she was finished getting her team together, the makeup of people who reported directly to her had changed dramatically—by more than 70 percent. But the results were good. The Workplace 2000 team had a lot of credibility, both as a group and as individuals with fresh ideas and deep inside knowledge.

The advantage that comes from working with people who have a deep understanding of the business may seem trivial—even irritating—but it isn't. Many change efforts have completely collapsed because the natural resistance to change was not smoothed through the understanding and inclusion necessary to help difficult ideas gain traction.

The Shared Values Needed for Successful Resurgence

Before we move on to discuss alternative approaches to coalition building, we want to hammer home some of the things that

Alberto-Culver, Harley-Davidson, Marshfield DoorSystems, and Motorola had in common. These very different companies built their change coalitions in very different ways. Yet when we look closer at these organizations and listen to their people talk about what really mattered at the time, we see a consistent focus on values and people.

At this early stage, the companies did not know what change would look like. To paraphrase the Alberto-Culver executive above, one of the first things the coalition had to do there—and at the other companies we saw—was to identify the real issues. But the coalition members all agreed that their individual companies had lost their way with the market. And the emphasis for everyone at this stage of the game was culture and values. How do we work together to solve this problem? How do we communicate what is wrong and work to fix it? How do we operate as a team, bringing different viewpoints in and integrating them? How do we ensure that everyone, regardless of where they sit in the organization, feels equally important and valued? It may seem soft, but those were the terms used by the people involved in change at the time. Their emphasis was not yet on the concrete manifestations of change but on the softer issues of culture and involvement. They agreed that they needed to change and that everyone inside the organization had to be involved.

WHEN OUTSIDERS DOMINATE

When it came to building their change coalitions, not every company put the same emphasis on people who had long-standing and known authority. Some approached the change process by instead embracing outside views and perspectives, either by hiring consultants to lead the change effort, or by building a change coalition out of new hires with specific functional expertise.

It can seem logical to add an outside perspective to any change effort. Company veterans are, after all, most vulnerable to the same denial and "God-given right" perspectives that prevent companies from embracing change. Even when veterans recognize the need for change, they might not be able to break through the traditional views, habits of mind, and false assumptions that led their firm to stagnate in the first place.

Consider as well the organizational dynamics that are in place when change begins. The struggling companies we observed were not, as a rule, cooperative or collaborative. The daily modus operandi in these places was to jockey for position in the ongoing multilateral turf wars that dominated in-house engagement. For some of them, turning to outside help from consultants or new hires seemed like a way to cut across functional boundaries and bypass those parts of the organization that were intent on disrupting change.

The leader who recognizes the need for change likewise may not control enough of the organization to be able to effect change on a multilateral level. He or she may feel that the only way to make change happen is to incubate it with an offstage effort and then bring it back in as a fait accompli.

Some combination of these issues was operating at the pseudonymous companies MediaCo, BenefitsInc, and EquipmentCo, each of which took the outside approach to coalition building.

MediaCo, for example, underwent some leadership turmoil in the early stages of its change efforts. A rival executive tried to execute a leveraged buyout and oust the CEO, a seasoned media executive we refer to as Bob Smith, whose vision of a more market-focused MediaCo was opposed by the other leader. The executive who attempted the LBO lost the fight and left MediaCo to become the CEO of another firm, clearing the way for Bob Smith to build his coalition out of the supporters who remained.

After the departure of the other executive, Bob Smith began to settle down into his role as a promoter of change. Smith saw that the growth of the Internet and the drop in traditional advertising revenue was creating a need for his organization to reinvent itself. He initiated an in-house change effort in the late 1990s and brought in a new vice president of strategy to help him change the firm's direction. But his coalition building stopped there.

According to one professional at MediaCo at the time, the leadership team was largely focused on relationships and sales. Its members did not share Smith's focus on production, continuous improvement, and processes.

The informant said, "[Bob] came from a company that was very accountable for results, but it didn't translate here. . . . I think he's really bright, but I think that he tended to rely on people who had been in place in these industries or in these segments for decades and they talked about how it's all about the relationship, it's all about our sales force . . . and I don't know if [Bob] saw, at least up front, all the things that he needed to change."

Smith's coalition-building efforts stopped short of creating a like-minded team that shared his market-focused view of how the business needed to change. Bob Smith may have been making changes, but his direct reports were pursuing business as usual.

When Consultants Substitute for Coalitions

In the wake of the leadership turmoil, Bob Smith may not have had the leadership authority to effect change outside his immediate circle. He wanted change, but the people around him did not.

The authority and credibility of the leader and the coalition team are crucial. Harley-Davidson, Marshfield DoorSystems, and even Alberto-Culver's change coalitions could effect change in large part because the members were insiders who were considered credible by the broader organization. These people had a deep, known investment in the success of the firms they were tasked with transforming.

Credibility is hugely important, and very difficult for outsiders to achieve in a short time frame, if at all. This may explain why, in our experience, change efforts do not go far when they are led by outside consulting groups.

BenefitsInc experienced this difficulty. BenefitsInc did not take steps to create a broad, cross-functional coalition for change. Instead, the BenefitsInc leader who recognized the need for market-focused change hired an external consulting firm to lead a branding effort. The reasons for this were opportunistic—the change executive did not have enough broad power in the company to effect wholesale change, so he was hoping to create change on a small scale in an area he controlled and then export it to other areas. He benefited from the fact that BenefitsInc had merged ten years earlier with another large company in the benefits space, so the rebranding was viewed as appropriate, even overdue, at the time.

The BenefitsInc executive gave the branding consultant sole ownership of the effort. The consultant ran with it, developing ideas without seeking much ongoing input from different functions within BenefitsInc. The consultant made no attempt to build a coalition inside the business. Instead, the leader tried to import change, fully formed, with a group of consultants—not internal advocates—as authors.

Not surprisingly, when the brand rolled out to the firm as a whole there was no change in behavior, no broader corporate values or behaviors that were promoted, and no internal ownership of what the brand meant and how the firm's team members could contribute.

The companies that hired consultants to assist in the change effort all made that same mistake—they let the consultants *be* the coalition. They didn't build their own in-house change team, so there was no one to take what the consultants did and make it their own.

Consultants can of course be an important component in the change effort. Consultants are effective at guiding the change process, among other roles. But successful change is more likely when the company uses consultants strategically and integrates the value that consultants add while maintaining ownership of the process. We frankly do not see many companies do that. From our experience, the leaders in charge of troubled companies delegate too much of the change effort to the consultant and fail to take real ownership. They fail to recognize that change requires the organization to own the change, and as a result they don't do the work to ensure that the efforts of consultants are ultimately embraced by the organization.

Marketers Hired to Reach Markets

Another common approach to coalition building is to focus on bringing in outside skills that the organization lacks, often in the area of marketing. Leading a market-focused resurgence requires, clearly, knowledge of the market. Many companies that slip into stagnation find that they do not actually know their markets well, nor do they have the people with the skills to learn more about their markets. A number of companies we studied recognized this gap and in the early days of change hired marketing personnel with the expectation that their knowledge would effect the change process. Some even thought that bringing in marketing people might make the entire change process unnecessary.

Just as consultants did not make for effective coalitions, the companies that built a kind of proxy coalition out of new hires with functional skills did not get the full benefit of that new knowledge and those new resources. The reasons were similar in that the new hires were not usually integrated into the company and into the change process.

BenefitsInc, for example, hired a number of new marketing personnel at around the same time that it launched its rebranding effort with the outside consultant (both efforts were inside the domain of the change leader). The rationale for hiring them was to improve the company's ability to connect with the market and interpret market shifts in consistent and relevant ways.

Sadly, few of these employees were successful at that task— through no fault of their own. They were neither vested with any inherent authority nor made part of a formal change coalition, so there was no real incentive for anyone else within the company to listen to them or change their behavior as a result of ideas they shared. These marketing team members were hired and placed in different departments, but their efforts were not integrated into the firm's culture or approach.

Not surprisingly, these people rarely lasted. One of the few marketers who stayed remarked, ten years later, "We continue to hire people from outside. They continue to leave on their own or they get fired. But it's a very difficult environment to work in if you're a real marketing person. . . . People were brought in and they said, 'You're here because we want you to initiate change.' And then [the marketers] tried to do that, and [management] said, 'Oops, sorry, we didn't really mean that—you're gone.'" The lack of support from top management and the absence of any shared understanding of the market caused the "outside" approach to fizzle and fade.

The investments made by BenefitsInc in its branding and marketing efforts were not entirely without benefit, however. A number of people hired during that period of change did manage to stay with the firm. That group eventually integrated the corporate branding effort, which many insiders claimed helped the firm become marginally more market-focused. But the company did not fully realize change, a fact which can be traced to the early failure to create a cohesive, authoritative change coalition.

CONCLUSION

Once leaders recognize the need for change, they start the difficult task of building a change coalition to lead the change effort. Effective change coalitions, in our experience, comprise people who have a shared set of values concerning the importance of the employees and the need to have a collaborative, cooperative culture in which people work together to find solutions. Members of the change coalition also have authority within the organization—people throughout the business view them as having a personal investment in the survival of the business as a whole.

In our experience, leaders who either failed to build a coalition or tried to patchwork one together with outside resources and new hires were not able to realize a successful market-focused reinvention. These outside forces were in a very real sense rejected by the organization, their views discarded as irrelevant to the company.

From coalitions come visions. In the next step, the change coalitions begin to develop a more formal vision of what change should look like.

REINVENT

4

A VISION FOR CHANGE

ONCE BILL BLANKENSHIP AND JERRY MANNIGEL HAD their Marshfield DoorSystems change coalition in place, they assembled coalition members to create a vision for change.

Marshfield DoorSystems is a custom provider in the door market. Marshfield sells to contractors and developers, not through retailers like Lowes or Home Depot. Their products vary in look, feel, weight, handles, materials, and dozens of other specifications. All Marshfield DoorSystems products are custom-built for specific buildings and projects, and creating fully custom doors is an enterprise-wide activity. So the reinvention under way at Marshfield DoorSystems really needed a vision for change that took into account the *processes* used within the company, and the people who used them. In short, that vision needed to serve the more than six hundred hourly union workers constructing doors in their plants; the dozens of sales and sales support people making promises about the product; and even the contractors who bought Marshfield products.

Given this context, it should be no surprise that when the coalition team emerged from early meetings with what they referred to as a "road map" for change, it was strikingly different from what many imagine would come out of a strategy meeting. The Marshfield DoorSystems road map highlighted six key points of focus for the company's market-focused resurgence.

1. Value Proposition and Value Delivery Systems: reinventing the business based on market needs
2. Communication Systems: all employees and managers know about the business, the markets, and change progress
3. Safety: care for employees
4. High-Performance Work Systems: continuous improvement in the organization
5. Organizational Alignment: clarity about roles, responsibilities, and relationships with the rest of the organization
6. Information Technology: tools to manage order complexity

Marshfield DoorSystems' vision is notable in a few ways. First, it says a lot about the importance of customers. The first item on the change list was to reinvent the company based on market needs—the market is the purpose and driver of the business.

Second, we were struck by how Marshfield identified the need to fundamentally change the approach to communication within the organization, so that every employee had the same understanding of the business and whom it serves. In our experience, few companies acknowledge broken systems so explicitly in their change plans.

The Marshfield vision is also notable, perhaps, for what it doesn't say. It says nothing about revenue targets or goals for units shipped. It says nothing about market share or what place it will hold relative to its competitors. Instead, the road map for Marshfield focused largely on the internal approaches and processes the company needed to become more responsive to the external needs of the market.

At a very deep level, this road map is about the way the work is done and the environment, or culture, in which that work happens. The vision defined the kind of company Marshfield DoorSystems wanted to be, one with a value proposition for the customer, open communication, a safe environment for employees, clear roles, a culture of continuous improvement, and the necessary tools for consistent, accurate order and inventory management. From this vision for change, the company embarked on a multiyear change effort that transformed the company from a limping concern, suffering millions in losses on its more than $50 million in revenue, into a strong growth company with sales in 2001 of more than $120 million with $10 million in profit.

WHAT DO YOU WANT TO BE?

The idea that companies need a "vision" has gained enormous popularity since the mid-1990s, helped by the evangelism of change guru John Kotter, as well as by Jim Collins and Jerry Porras.[1] Few would argue with the logic: how could you or your employees possibly know what they are working toward without some kind of vision?

Creating a vision marks the first step in the second stage of change: Reinvent (see Figure 4-1). At this point in the change

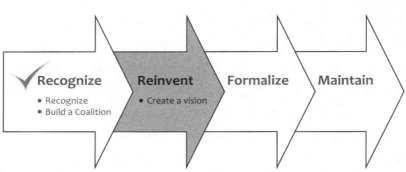

Figure 4-1: **Reinvent: The First Step Is to Create a Vision**

process the coalition gets much more concrete about what specific changes need to occur. These changes emphasize and even define the environment of the firm, explicitly identifying the behaviors and norms that are acceptable within the desired culture.

A useful *vision for change* looks remarkably different from what many businesses understand a corporate vision should be; it even looks different from what most management experts promote. John Kotter suggests that a change vision should essentially promote "a sensible and appealing picture of the future," which includes an imagined future set of goals.[2]

As attractive as it sounds, a relevant "end-state" vision can be difficult to create in practice, especially at the start of a change effort. Alberto-Culver's Carol Bernick confessed about the days and weeks after she recognized the need for change that "I had no idea how much it would take, and I had little idea what I would even do." The problem can seem very complex and distant, overwhelmed by the immediate, everyday needs of selling products, serving customers, and running operations.

Struggling companies that develop any kind of plan at all often tend to create "visions" that are really just an articulation of ways to stop the bleeding. Losing market share? Focus your change efforts on sales. No new products in the pipeline? Focus change on R & D.

Unfortunately, such outcome-driven visions alone frequently fail to bring results. Again, they focus too much on what individual functions of the organization can do, and the desired changes are sought too soon, long before the change coalition understands the market and the available capabilities the firm has to satisfy customers.

Alternatively, companies may be inspired by the advice of Collins and Porras to define "purpose" and "values." Values are critical to business success—as we discussed in the previous chapter, one of the marks of an effective change coalition is that its members have a shared set of values. But language like "We provide superior customer service" is at once too universal (no company aims to provide *inferior* customer service) and too generic (individual employees can have very different conceptions of what it means in practice). For the purposes of change, the vision and the way it articulates or reflects the firm's values need to be more specific.

We have consistently seen that companies leading a successful resurgence drove change with a vision that explicitly addressed the way things are done in the firm. Overwhelmingly, the change vision strongly pursued change to the company's *processes* and how those processes establish and reinforce cultural values and norms concerning communication and collaboration, and the firm's relationship to the market.

CULTURE DEFINES COMMUNICATION

Alberto-Culver North America was a multimillion-dollar company when Carol Bernick became its president. But it still functioned in many ways as the family-run company her father had started forty years earlier. Leonard Lavin liked to be the one with the good ideas. He traveled around the world in his capacity as an entrepreneur, and then came back to headquarters with ideas for new products or product tweaks. This entrepreneurial approach worked to grow the firm into a multimillion-dollar enterprise, but it also created a strictly hierarchical structure in which Lavin made all the decisions.

One senior executive described the environment by saying, "In what I would say the late eighties, early nineties, when I was first with the company, it was very much a top-down structure. Mr. Lavin was very much in control of the consumer products division in terms of very much driving what he thought was appropriate innovation and appropriate new ideas. It was more of a quarter-to-quarter business, where, literally, the horizon for new products was very quick and in all honesty I don't know how much real external data they were getting, other than his visits either around the world or, I mean, a lot of this was truly entrepreneurial as far as where the ideas were coming from. Basically, the company waited around to be told what to do by Leonard Lavin."

In Lavin's defense, such centralized control is very common in companies with an entrepreneurial genius founder. Apple's Steve Jobs was famous in the early years of the company for brutally dismissing an employee's idea, only to come back a week later to present it as his own—often to the person who pitched it to him in the first place. In the case of Alberto-Culver, no one but Lavin was authorized to pursue good ideas that didn't come from the top. As a result, people working two or three levels down often had no idea about the direction of the business.

The hierarchical structure persisted after Lavin stepped down, breeding dissatisfaction in the mature Alberto-Culver. Worse, it created a lot of misunderstanding about what the business did and where it made its money. Alberto-Culver's best-known and best-selling brand in terms of units at the time that Bernick took over was VO5, the line of hair treatment and conditioning products. But VO5 earned Alberto-Culver only a penny per bottle in profit. The real profit generator was Sally Beauty Supply, a chain of retail beauty supply stores. Sally Beauty, despite its profit impact, was widely viewed in-house as a "side" business.

Broken internal communications and conflicting views about what was important to the business are almost universal in struggling companies. At MediaCo, philosophical differences between the sales and operations sides of the business bred mistrust and created an environment in which people actively smiled and agreed with each other, but acted narrowly and individually when it came to day-to-day management.

BenefitsInc had similar problems that stemmed from the fact that the company had formed through a merger of two smaller companies; a decade later, its employees still identified with the original, pre-merger businesses from which they had come, a dynamic reinforced by the fact that everyone tended to communicate and collaborate only with others in their location (all of whom had also worked for the original merger participant). The lack of cooperative work with people in other locations made it hard to identify others as part of the same team.

Harley-Davidson suffered broken and dysfunctional communication based on the company's historical emphasis on design and engineering. By the time Harley began its change effort, the product development process had a group of isolated designers creating a look and feel that the engineers would then modify to accommodate function and fit. Neither group sought input from other parts of the company, nor were they engaging in true collaboration with each other. They just did their work and then passed it along to operations. "If you go back to the seventies," one informant said, "it was more of an 'over the wall' process, where engineering designed the things and threw them over the wall. . . ." Harley-Davidson also struggled due to a tense relationship with the union, a fairly common problem. The animosity was so strong that Harley kept financial information a secret from union officials.

But perhaps the most dramatic example of dysfunctional communication comes from Motorola, where communication between business units was intentionally nonexistent. Since its inception, Motorola was an engineering-driven company that deeply valued the discovery and innovation of new inventions. For much of its history during the twentieth century, there were no external forces pushing the company to bring better products to market. Motorola had earned 80 percent market share in mobile phones mainly because it had no serious external competition.

To keep its edge and create an incentive for its engineers to improve products and bring new ideas to market, the PCS business unit needed to challenge *itself*. So it developed a deeply competitive culture in which product groups were pitted against each other to come up with the next best thing. Most companies think about trade secrets as the innovations and research you keep out of the hands of competitors, and it's true that Motorola had draconian policies for protecting proprietary information. But other product groups were also treated as if they were rivals like Nokia. Different businesses were described by some as "warring tribes." The result was a deeply siloed, deeply competitive, and deeply suspicious culture that served as a liability when the cellular phone market began to disrupt Motorola's historical dominance.

Regardless of the historical cause, the communications breakdowns experienced by struggling companies often evolve out of deeply hierarchical, siloed, noncollaborative cultures in which employees have a very limited perspective on the larger whole or how to affect it. One Marshfield DoorSystems executive said of the state of communication in the firm, "These people have been managed heavily by the mushroom theory: kept in the dark and fed a lot of shit."

The lack of communication is rarely as intentional as it was at Motorola. Some of the organizations we spent time with *tried* to communicate with their employees, but the communication was so infrequent and unfocused that it had little or no meaning. For instance, at Alberto-Culver financial information was shared with employees on a quarterly basis when it was publicly announced, but the corporate financial statements didn't give a sense of progress on a group, product, or market level; and because information was parsed out internally according to functions, people often couldn't see how everything fit together or why certain measures mattered. Assembling the larger picture was virtually impossible, even if all the parts were shared.

Failure to address these cultural issues, and their resulting effects on communications, will stymie a firm's resurgence. Broken communications are easy to ignore or justify or dismiss as "normal," but in the end, communication issues seep into the soil of the firm and breed a whole generation of related problems, including individualism, avoidance of collaboration, duplication, confusion over roles and responsibilities, and general ignorance of the customer.

This context of poor communications bred in through culture makes clear why change required the kind of process-oriented vision that Marshfield DoorSystems laid out. Its six-point road map explicitly addressed the cultural dysfunction it had bred as an organization and what deserved its focused attention. Suffice it to say, that road map was exactly what Marshfield DoorSystems needed at the time. For others pursuing market-focused resurgence an explicit focus on creating a culture of communication allows many other challenges to come into line.

USING PROCESSES TO CHANGE CULTURE

We can see how a focus on its culture and mechanisms of communication bred change at Alberto-Culver. Once Carol Bernick had her Workplace 2000 change coalition in place, she tasked them with coming up with suggestions to directly address the cultural issues at the company.

The result was the initiation of a program within the company called the Growth Development Leader, or GDL. As one informant explained it, the GDL program had three essential goals: communication, teamwork, and workplace efficiency. A GDL was a person who served as a kind of cultural ambassador for a group or business unit. Each GDL was assigned to about thirty people with whom they would communicate core company messages. GDLs met with Carol Bernick multiple times during the year to hear her views on the direction of the company and to bring suggestions from the employees straight to the top. Most corporate information was likewise sent to employees through the GDL network. GDLs also served as coaches and mentors to the people in their group and otherwise provided support.

Curiously, a person's GDL was not necessarily his or her boss. One informant explained the logic of this distinction: "We felt that managers were great 'thing' managers: projects, things. But not, on average, great people managers."

When it first implemented the program, Alberto-Culver asked for people to volunteer to serve as GDLs. From a pool of candidates, the Workplace 2000 team chose people known for having very strong people skills, communication ability, and a teamwork mentality. They also had to be able to juggle multiple responsibilities with grace—the GDL role was not the only responsibility these people had, so they all had to serve in this capacity and still deliver on their "day jobs."

Alberto-Culver put the GDL program into place with the intention of training and developing existing operational managers to take on GDL responsibilities over time. Over two years, the company trained its operational managers in the techniques and approaches necessary to cultivate effective communication and collaboration in the organization.

Motorola's Vision for Change:
Collaborative Values Reinforced through Process

Motorola took an entirely different approach to planning for change, albeit one that was, eventually, appropriate for its challenges and historical divisions. Motorola's change efforts did not progress in a smooth line. The company experienced a number of bumps and restarts along the way. The challenge came because Motorola's first attempts to create change did not progress from recognition to coalition building and then the creation of a vision.

Instead, once there was recognition of the need for change, the change leader, Chris Galvin, jumped in with a number of separate initiatives aimed at cultivating a greater market orientation in the business. For example, early in the change process Motorola initiated corporate-sponsored training for hundreds of senior executives, and it hired a number of seasoned marketing professionals to beef up the firm's skills in traditional marketing techniques, such as segmentation.

These efforts did little to stop Motorola from struggling. Again, the problem lay with the culture. At the risk of understatement, Motorola was not a company that valued marketing. There was a favorite saying among Motorola engineers that marketing was where failed engineers went to die. Marketing, in that culture, was a place for people who couldn't make it in the functions that *mattered*. Efforts to improve Motorola's marketing abilities were successful. It hired a few marketing experts, who produced better segmentation and branding efforts. But that work did nothing to address the core problems of broken communication and cultural isolation.

"We learned pretty quickly that it wasn't a knowledge thing, necessarily," one informant said. "You actually had a bunch of people that were running around with Kellogg MBAs, who already got this stuff, and were just beating their heads up against the walls saying, 'It isn't that we don't know how to do marketing—we're not *allowed* to do it.'"

We have said that sequence matters, and Motorola clearly shows why, because these early efforts actually created more division within the company. By hiring more marketers, Motorola management sent the unintended message that the change efforts happening within the company would benefit the *marketing* function. This prospect met with a great deal of resistance from those who clung to Motorola's traditional engineering and entrepreneurial orientations, and served to solidify the sense of conflict and broken communication between groups that supported a move toward greater market orientation and those that did not. Motorola PCS's global market share continued to decline, hitting a low for the time of 14.6 percent in 2000.

The real turnaround began with the arrival of Mike Zafirovski, who was hired from GE to be the head of the PCS division. Even before he arrived, Motorola CEO Chris Galvin had realized that he had not gone far enough to realize change. It became clear to Galvin at that point that the business needed to put more emphasis on culture—and less on functional marketing—as part of its change effort. When Zafirovski arrived he formed a change coalition. The vision for Motorola's resurgence that came from that team emphasized a set of guiding values that would be reinforced with high-level investment in two processes.

The values were cribbed from GE's "4E's" model of leadership—energy, energizer, edge, execution. Zafirovski added a fifth—ethics. At the same time that Zafirovski was communicating about those values and promoting them in the PCS division, he put forth a vision for change that emphasized the use of two process-oriented frameworks that encouraged—even forced—communication and cross-functional teamwork: Six Sigma and M-Gate.

Six Sigma is the famed quality and improvement methodology created by Motorola. M-Gate is a staged-gate product development process that the Motorola Land Mobile business unit—the part of the company responsible for wireless infrastructure and semiconductors, among other products—had been using as part of its effort to become more market-focused, and which Zafirovski adopted for the PCS unit. M-Gate was by definition cross-functional—engineering could not move a product to the next phase without collaboration and buy-in from a number of other functions, including design and marketing.

By emphasizing a set of core values and creating a plan that focused on processes and practices consistent with these values, Zafirovski and his change coalition forced the formation of cross-functional teams, and encouraged broad ownership and understanding of initiatives across the organization.

This emphasis on collaboration was key to change not only at Motorola but at Harley, where the change coalition put high emphasis on implementing collaborative processes in the weeks and months after the LBO. Specifically, Harley-Davidson worked to increase employee involvement in internal problem solving and in getting closer to the customers; to implement just-in-time inventory to cut down on inventories and to conserve capital; and to implement statistical operator control, in which every employee was trained. Although informants emphasized that their greatest challenge after the LBO was staying in business, all of them believed that the guiding coalition was focused on a plan to fundamentally change how Harley-Davidson operated.

VALUES NEED TO BE DRIVEN, NOT JUST DEFINED

Alberto-Culver, Harley-Davidson, Marshfield DoorSystems, and Motorola put heavy emphasis on values and culture as critical to the change vision. Values also played a role in defining the change vision at MediaCo and EquipmentCo. There was an important difference, however, in how values came into the conversation at these companies. It was not an internal, organic evolution but one brought from without.

Leaders at both MediaCo and EquipmentCo realized that their companies did not have the abilities in-house to navigate their own resurgence. Both companies engaged Senn-Delaney Leadership Consulting Group, an organizational development firm with an excellent reputation for helping companies navigate the change process. The consulting firm provided the framework for cultural change and training services and materials that MediaCo and EquipmentCo took advantage of in later stages. (We discuss the role of training in Chapter 6.)

Early in their engagement, Senn-Delaney consultants worked with executives and managers in both companies to define the organizational values they perceived as essential for their firms' success. The EquipmentCo parent company, HoldingsInc, identified its seven core values as: (1) respect for people; (2) customer focus; (3) relentless pursuit of quality in all we do; (4) speed, simplicity, agility; (5) innovation; (6) accountability; and (7) communication.

Senn-Delaney helped MediaCo's senior management develop a similar set of values when it went through the same exercise in 1999 to develop both a new mission statement and cultural values. MediaCo's five key values, accompanied by shortened catchphrases used internally, were: (1) leadership through the relentless pursuit of excellence ("own the results"); (2) customer intimacy and insight ("be a partner"); (3) respect for all, integrity always ("be open be honest"); (4) one team committed to common goals ("get there together"); and (5) leading change through innovation ("define the future"). Once the values were in place, MediaCo crafted a change plan framed as: "change our business model; change our processes and organization; change our culture; [and] change how we go to market."

When these companies focused on the kind of culture and values they needed to achieve the change they wanted, all named strikingly similar values and norms. In fact, when we look across the organizations we have observed, there are six values identified *by all of them* as necessary for a market-focused resurgence (see Figure 4-2).

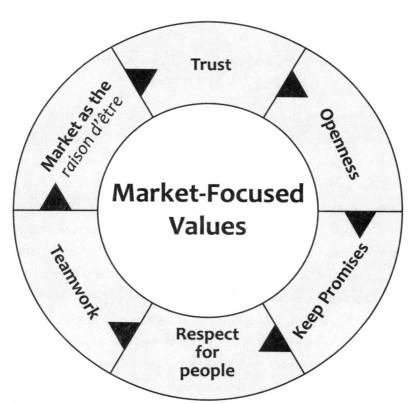

Figure 4-2:   The Common Values of Market-Focused Firms

Regardless of whether their change efforts ultimately worked out, the companies that embark on market-focused change all broadly agree on the values they needed to be successful. The values defined by all these organizations were important for setting the stage for change. So what makes the difference? If MediaCo, BenefitsInc, and EquipmentCo identified the same values as Alberto-Culver and others, why didn't they see the same results?

The difference lay in the fact that they defined the values but the values did not become integrated into the organization's culture. As we will show in the next section, as well as in the next two chapters, the change in explicit values did not result in consistent, explicit behavior change, nor were there any consequences for not adhering to the new values. Employees—and, more importantly, leaders—behaved no differently.

CHANGE VISIONS FOCUS ON THE MARKET, NOT MARKETING

As the stories of the seven companies we spent time with make clear, there are some common circumstances within struggling firms and some common approaches that are necessary to set the stage for a market-oriented resurgence. All these businesses were culturally hierarchical with dysfunctional communications systems, and all of them developed plans in the early stages of their resurgence to alter the cultural norms. Instead of isolation, they sought teamwork. Instead of secrecy or obfuscation, they hoped for clear communication.

Many companies understand the importance of process and culture in creating resurgence, but the commitment to those processes and culture was inconsistent. In some cases, there seemed to be real and deep confusion over what it meant to be *market-*focused. In a number of companies, a mistranslation occurred.

Leaders were trying to build process-focused plans for change with a focus on shifting the culture. But the message that was received was a shift to *marketing*-focused rather than *market*-focused. The significant investments that a number of businesses were making in the marketing function—most notably BenefitsInc—added to the confusion about the nature and emphasis of change and who was slated to benefit.

Few of the marketing personnel whom BenefitsInc hired stayed very long. They were rejected by the organization, frustrated by the difficulty they faced overcoming organizational resistance to change. Consider for a minute what those people were probably up against. Word got around BenefitsInc early on that change was afoot, but the message that made its way through the organization was that the change was to become more *marketing*-oriented. Employees would interpret that as more siloed managerial maneuvering, in which one department would be advantaged over others. The functions that stood to lose stature from such a shift would, of course, resist, and thus all good ideas and positive shifts that marketing could bring got rejected before they could take hold. The same fate awaited the corporate rebranding effort that BenefitsInc hoped would create a new identity and a new aspirational marker for the merged firm (already ten years old at the time).

The experience at BenefitsInc is illustrative of what can happen when businesses confuse *marketing* with *market*-focused change. The branding coalition at BenefitsInc sought to implement change by developing a new brand identity without the involvement of the business units. The company hoped the new brand identity would create a greater market focus, as members of the organization sought to live up to the aspirational nature of the brand. Yet there was very little formally done to teach people how to be more market-focused. As a result, the branding team was marginalized, defined as "communications"—a peripheral designation at BenefitsInc—and not perceived as having any important authority for change. A member of the team described the situation at the time:

> [The initial branding effort] was a very compartmentalized one. A little bit like, "We have a sore throat, let's do everything we need to get rid of that sore throat," not realizing that maybe that sore throat is representative of something really bad in your lungs. So we put all of our energy into the sore throat. That energy was "the way we present ourselves externally." We did not think . . . or did not openly discuss, I should say, that if you change your suit of clothes, it's going to mean that people are going to expect different things of you. My fear at the time, we all had this sense, all of us that were on this project, that this could be the most significant thing that happens to this company; but compartmentalize the way you sell this in, because if you make it bigger than it needs to be early on, you scare people off. So we emphasized that "okay, we have this icon as opposed to the old one and we're gonna say we're looking out for employees' best interests, people are going to expect all sorts of things." It's going to mean that we have to serve people differently; it means we have to treat each other differently. All of the sudden, anytime I started to get into those kinds of discussions, the pushback I would get was "That's not your job. Your job is communications." So I'm thinking, "You know what? They're actually giving some very good advice on how to get this done. So focus just on the cosmetics. It's going to look great, it's going to be a better feel and what not." But instinctively, we knew there could be an issue. . . .

BenefitsInc sabotaged itself. By trying to create change that was nonthreatening, it marginalized and minimized the importance of the only substantial change effort it initiated. By keeping the change efforts offstage, housed with a branding team brought in for the purpose, they ensured that no one inside the business would own or feel invested in its outcome.

Avon and the Marketing Trap

BenefitsInc is certainly not the only business we have seen concentrate its efforts to become more market-focused on, reductively, marketing. Avon, the famed beauty brand, has been in the news in recent months for its failed turnaround. The analysis all points to the evidence that Andrea Jung—Avon's CEO since 1999—pursued change by leaning too heavily on her marketing tool kit.

Jung had amassed a reputation as a genius retail marketer from years of working for brands like Neiman Marcus and Bloomingdale's. Avon's prior CEO, Jim Preston, had first hired Jung to do a feasibility study on placing Avon products in department stores. Jung's conclusion at the time was that the strategy wouldn't work—Avon did not have the packaging or the brand position to compete with the brands common to department stores, such as Clinique, Clarins, and MAC, to name a few.

Preston was so impressed by Jung's insights that he hired her in 1994 to lead the US consumer product division. She was promoted to COO, despite having no operations experience, and in 1999 given the role of chief executive.

Over the next four years Avon enjoyed strong growth, earning a market valuation of $21 billion in 2003. Jung's approach during the first four years of her tenure was to emphasize a new image both for the modern market of beauty-conscious, value-savvy women product buyers and for the small- and micro-entrepreneurial Avon Ladies who sell the products. Jung changed the company tagline from the famous "Ding dong, Avon calling" to "The company for women," which became the focus of the company's first global advertising campaign. Tennis stars Serena and Venus Williams were signed as spokespeople, and advertising spending rose dramatically. The company also entered a number of international markets, such as Brazil and, later, China.

But the biggest surprise came when Jung began to push Avon to adopt a more traditional distribution model by selling through retailers—the same model Jung had rejected ten years before. Granted, ten years is a long time, but little seemed to have changed. Avon's recognition and status were grounded in the iconic Avon Lady, the empowered, independent businesswoman selling her wares to other empowered, independent women. That image didn't translate to mall kiosks and JCPenney. Within a few years Avon abandoned the retail effort. But the company was weakened and unfocused. Over the subsequent eight years it re-organized and reorganized again, launching still more marketing efforts without trying to understand the core customer and what she got from Avon.

Jung certainly recognized that Avon needed change, and she likely pulled together a group of people around her who supported her view of the world. But the vision she developed for the company was largely outcome-driven, buttressed by bold financial pre-dictions that were not grounded in real connection to the market and what it wanted. For example, Jung announced a "Road to $20 Billion" plan that envisioned a doubling of revenue in five years, but a cohesive, process-oriented vision, a plan for execution, and a description of the organization's next incarnation were never devel-oped and shared among stakeholders throughout the company. The vision was mainly just a marketing vision, driven by Jung's market-ing prowess and rubber-stamped by an overly supportive board.

Market-Focused, Not World-Class Marketing

The instinct to hire marketing people to create market-oriented change seems to stem partly from a deep misunderstanding of the difference between marketing as a function and *the market*. The temptation is great, as marketing seems clear, concrete, and manageable. "The market," by contrast, is amorphous, changeable. It is no surprise that confusion would erupt even within respected, industry-leading companies.

EquipmentCo also invested significantly in the marketing function. EquipmentCo began its change efforts by forming a change coalition with representation across the company's leadership. But despite the input it received from Senn-Delaney, the ultimate plan it developed for change focused on becoming, as one informant put it, "kind of a world-class marketing organization."

Despite that emphasis, EquipmentCo did not invest the marketing department with the authority and stature consistent with its goals. The same informant noted that "marketing is not a high-level position within the company. So we don't have strong marketing leadership, if you will . . . [and] the marketing directors at the production centers have dotted-line responsibilities into the GMs, but they report to the VP of marketing, who is below the VP/GMs. So it's not an organization structure that is conducive to making us be that world-class marketing company."

MediaCo experienced similar challenges with its marketing-focused change plan. Early in the change effort, MediaCo CEO Bob Smith resurrected the corporate marketing council, a cross-functional body comprised of marketing representatives from each business group. Earlier incarnations of the corporate marketing council had been formed and abandoned due to lack of interest and investment on the part of the participating representatives, who still reported and were accountable to their business unit presidents, who generally did not believe in or support the council. Bob Smith's vision did not break through this organizational prejudice. Unit marketing representatives eventually abandoned Smith's council as well once they saw that it lacked legitimacy, authority, and influence in the corporation.

We don't want to give the impression that these companies are somehow foolish or naïve to take this approach. In fact, at BenefitsInc and elsewhere they knew that taking a *marketing*-focused approach to creating change would not produce the full range of results they wanted. They knew the marketing function tasked with steering change was not vested with enough authority to make change happen. Yet these companies either were not prepared or didn't think it was feasible to tackle the culture and cultural norms of the business as a way to set the stage for change. To paraphrase the informant from BenefitsInc, they don't want to "scare people off." But the result is that the business spends significant time, money, and human potential on an approach that categorically will not be successful. Successful change cannot come from *marketing*-oriented moves.

EBAY'S VISION: RETHINKING THE CORE CUSTOMER

eBay was not one of the seven companies involved in our original study, but its status as a survivor of the 1990s Internet boom makes its recent experience with a change effort that began in 2008 a fascinating complement to the others we've seen.[3]

eBay's change efforts took off when John Donahoe, the current CEO, took over for Meg Whitman. Donahoe had been leading the "marketplace" side of the business, which is what eBay calls the flagship auction platform that Pierre Omidyar first created in the mid-1990s. When Donahoe took over, the auction house was showing signs of stagnation. Annual reports were no longer peppered with messages of meteoric growth. eBay had its dedicated sellers and buyers (both roles often played by the same person or merchant), but the number of new participants was static. A number of major acquisitions brought no new value and were divested—most notably, eBay acquired Skype in

2005 for more than $2 billion, an incredible sum considering Skype's unimpressive income at the time and general doubt in the market about the synergies between the VoIP provider and eBay's core business. eBay eventually divested its investment in Skype in stages, first to a group of investors and more recently to Microsoft.[4]

Donahoe recognized the need for change, and he worked to reshape the senior leadership team to reflect changes at the company. But when it came to creating a vision for change, eBay had a particular challenge compared to Alberto-Culver, Harley-Davidson, Marshfield DoorSystems, and Motorola in that its attention was split between serving two different primary "markets." For over ten years eBay's primary purpose had been to match buyers and sellers and then basically to get out of the way. The PayPal payments service offered a way for those parties to deal with the financial transaction, but everything else was left to the participants—shipping, dispute resolution, etc.

We would not go so far as to say eBay had *nothing* for the seller, but its service was simple by design. It established itself as a matchmaker at a time when online matchmaking was necessary. Indeed, in the years before traditional retailers established and executed on an ecommerce strategy, and before the population of Internet users became indistinguishable from the mass market, eBay's bazaar-like atmosphere, coupled with the excitement of bidding, generated high demand. But by 2008 the company's value proposition for the buyer was getting squeezed between the excellent, full-service online presence of Amazon and the excellent, specified offerings of online retailers such as homedepot.com. eBay's "Buy It Now" feature added convenience for customers who were happy to simply buy a product once found, but it also made eBay almost indistinguishable in function from Amazon, while maintaining the hassle of fulfillment.

eBay needed a vision for change that, like Marshfield's, aimed to "reinvent the business based on market needs." "We need to aggressively change our product, our customer approach, and our business model," Donahoe said in a conference call with investors early in his tenure.[5] But if all eBay had done was change the way it served its retail customer, it might have temporarily improved its position but would not have reinvented itself. Instead, eBay's resurgence required a vision that shifted its primary attention away from the buyer and toward the seller—the merchants and retailers using eBay to complement or even in lieu of an independent online presence.

At this stage in the maturation of the Internet, most companies with a commerce-oriented online presence understand how expensive and complex it can be to keep up with the ever-changing technology required to present your products in a way that buyers can find and buy them. Buyers, in contrast, need only a credit card and an Internet connection—or, today, a smartphone. eBay's vision for reinvention thus focused on the needier side of the equation, those online brick-and-mortar merchants that would gladly pay someone to figure out the technological requirements of ecommerce for them.

eBay's acquisition spree over the past five years reflects that vision of reinvention for the merchant market. It has bought Bill Me Later, a payments service that complements PayPal; GSI, an ecommerce software developer; and a number of mobile application developers. These added capabilities have led to a multifold increase in the number and scope of merchant-oriented services. These include a location-based app that lets the department store brand Macy's detect when a customer is close to the store and send coupons or promotions to woo him in; a triangular device called PayPal Here that small-scale or field-based merchants can attach to their mobile phones and use to swipe customer credit cards for payment; and an ecommerce development and hosting services—eBay currently runs more than five hundred ecommerce websites for established merchants, such as Godiva chocolatiers and Mattel.

There was plenty of cultural change needed to reflect that shift. The leadership turnover alone reflects that the mind-set and approach needed by a technology infrastructure company serving merchants are dramatically different from those required by a re-tail marketplace. The process is by no means over—eBay contin-ues to have ups and downs—but its story is notable for the vision for change it needed to emphasize merchants, and through them to better serve the retail customer.

CONCLUSION

Once the change coalition is in place, the company must begin its efforts to reinvent the firm. In the first step of the Reinvent stage, coalition members define a vision for change that focuses on the behaviors and processes needed to shift the culture away from the uncommunicative, siloed modus operandi to a more collaborative, team-based culture. Curiously, all the companies that embark on a market-focused resurgence define the same set of values that are necessary to shift the culture of their businesses. With this plan in place, leaders are ready to make a public statement of change to the broader organization.

STAGE II

REINVENT

5

GOING PUBLIC

THE EAGLE SOARS ALONE.

That was the theme of a Harley-sponsored ride that the thirteen new owners went on within months of closing the leveraged
buyout from AMF. The ride started on June 16, 1981, in York,
Pennsylvania, where eight years earlier Harley, then backed by
AMF, had opened a new manufacturing facility. Riders traveled
across the Midwest to Milwaukee, Wisconsin, Harley-Davidson's
historical and spiritual home and headquarters. Willie G. Davidson, grandson of Harley-Davidson's founder and a longtime product designer for the company, led the pack as the group traveled
across the central states and stopped periodically at dealerships
along the way. As Peter Reid recounted in his book *Well Made in
America,* one Harley-Davidson employee climbed to the roof of a

Pittsburgh Harley-Davidson dealership and used a can of black spray paint to block out the AMF logo.[1]

The message that the change coalition wanted to send to the Harley-Davidson organization and its union was clear: Harley-Davidson stands on its own now. More importantly, its new leadership is like *you*—motorcycle riders. This wasn't some investment bank or corporate takeover giant prepared to gut the company for its assets. These were people who cared about the company, its history, and the product it made, and they were there to represent that commitment. "The Eagle Stands Alone" slogan was printed on T-shirts and other swag and handed out at every opportunity. The entire event and its choreography were a conscious effort to say that things at Harley-Davidson would be different. The company was moving away from the era in York, where AMF doubled production and halved the level of quality, and added Ski-Doo snowmobile parts and other nontraditional Harley products to the mix.

One informant said of the event, "People were ecstatic that the company was becoming private. But there were a lot of people worried too. 'What was the future going to be like?' . . . I think it seems almost quaint now. It was pretty exciting! To see the company's owners all there together."

The credibility of the Harley-Davidson leadership is hard to overstate. Everyone we spoke to shared a positive perception of Vaughn Beals and his team. As one informant put it, "We had charismatic leaders then. Vaughn Beals, you should meet the guy. He is a tough man. He's like Norman Schwarzkopf; you want to follow the guy. Charlie Thompson of the P&A group was also very charismatic; he came from a dealer. Big, lovable-bear type of guy, but you knew he could be [tough]. You wanted to follow these people. It's almost like I felt hypnotized by the story. 'Sign me up! Consider me part of it!'"

GOING PUBLIC WITH CHANGE

The Harley-Davidson Eagle Soars Alone ride was not just a motorcycle ride or a publicity stunt, but a demarcation of change. The purpose of events such as these is to communicate the vision for change laid out by the coalition to the broader organization (see Figure 5-1). Up to this point, the change effort has been fairly limited to the change leader and the coalition members he or she nominates. But as soon as the vision has been defined and documented, the company then needs to communicate the vision to all employees and, in the case of Marshfield and Harley, to union workers. Demarcation events such as these serve to gather support and energy for the difficult effort that lies ahead. The message to all employees and stakeholders is clear on the point that everyone will need to be involved.

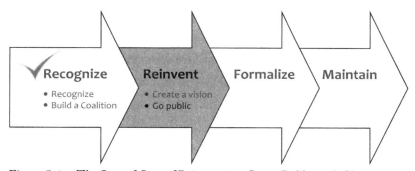

Figure 5-1:   The Second Step of Reinvention: Going Public with Change

Each company will find a different way or approach to communicating its intentions for change. Harley-Davidson chose an approach that went perfectly with its history—what better way to demonstrate what is important to the firm than to get everyone outside on a June ride? But the Harley-Davidson ride shared an important quality with other successful demarcation events we have seen. Namely, there was a clear and dramatic investment in performance. The event was high profile and public, and in it the company leaders made some clear, if tacit, commitments.

Leaders tend to be uncomfortable with these kinds of public performances. While they are expressly done to communicate with employees, the word can spread to other constituent groups. As a result, they create a public expectation for change, both the purpose and the source of the risk. Public announcements of change are, in one sense, a de facto admission of a mistake. Publicly admitting a mistake is difficult for any leader, and particularly risky for the leaders of publicly traded companies, whose every move is scrutinized by stockholders and Wall Street analysts. Sadly, no alternative, compared to a public demarcation event, has the same galvanizing effect.

Howard Schultz, the CEO of Starbucks, came to that conclusion in early 2008, shortly after he retook his position at the helm of the company. He had come back to steer the iconic coffee company through a difficult period of change. Among the challenges at Starbucks was a decrease in the consistency and quality of the coffee beverages served in its stores. Coffee connoisseurs know the flavor compounds in coffee are quite delicate. Pulling the perfect espresso shot requires the exact grind, set into the portafilter with an exact amount of pressure, and then brewed for an exact amount of time at an exact temperature. Too fast and you get a thin, weak espresso; too slow and the hot water can "burn" the ground coffee, producing a bitter beverage. So many Starbucks drinks were coming out with that bitter flavor that some coffee drinkers just assumed that was how Starbucks coffee tasted. Bitter coffee is just one of the reasons why Starbucks customers were being drawn at one end to the coffee offerings of chains like Dunkin' Donuts and McDonald's, and from the other to the artisanal purveyors like Peet's on the West Coast, La Colombe in Philadelphia, and Café Grumpy, Joe, the Art of Coffee, and a dozen other microchains in New York City and elsewhere. Under these pressures and others, Starbucks determined it needed to retrain its baristas to make sure they were using the right techniques. The only way to do that efficiently was to close all 7,100 Starbucks locations across the United States during serving hours and retrain them all at once.

Schultz writes in his book *Onward* that he knew of no other retail store that had ever taken such a drastic and public step, but he saw no choice. Yes, it was an admission to critics, competitors, investors, and other stakeholders that Starbucks had lost its edge. But it was also a clear commitment to Starbucks employees that the company was going to change and that they needed to be a part of it. Schultz writes, "If the espresso was not good enough, I told everyone . . . they had my permission to pour it out and begin again." That is a huge commitment to the people tasked with pulling shots for long lines of harried commuters.[2]

Another company that initiated a critical change effort during the mid-to-late 2000s is, ironically, McDonald's. In 2003, the company's board ousted the standing CEO, Jack Greenberg, and replaced him with retired McDonald's vice chairman Jim Cantalupo. The company was struggling under increased pressure from "fast casual" chains like Subway, which sells fast, healthy meals. The market, it seemed, had moved away from the Big Mac. To make matters worse, the McDonald's experience had declined, a challenge akin to Motorola slipping to number two. McDonald's made its name around the world as a place where middle-class families could go to enjoy a meal consistent in quality and price. It wasn't the best food you could get, but you knew what it was going to be. That pleasant, predictable experience had eroded by 2003. McDonald's restaurants were increasingly criticized as dirty, its staff as rude, its meals as poorly made or old.

Within months Cantalupo had assembled a change coalition and was going public with a vision for change that was referred to internally as the "Plan to Win." The plan focused on five P's: People, Products, Place, Price, Promotion. Criticized as overly cute and marketing-focused, the plan is considered sacred inside the company, and in practice it has been executed with a sincere focus on equipping employees to provide top service, and connecting with customers to make sure that McDonald's is offering the products and experience they want. The "Five P's" may have smacked too much of sloganeering, but a mnemonic works exactly because it is memorable. Cantalupo and his team were making a commitment, and they wanted to make sure everyone heard it.[3]

Such commitments are critical for successful change. Public promises like the one Howard Schultz made to retrain his employees prevent confusion. No one who worked for Harley-Davidson in June 1981, or for Starbucks in February 2008, could say later that their leaders were ambiguous about their intentions. Public events such as these are not just one-way communication vehicles. They present a clear choice to employees by saying, in clear terms, "We are doing this. You can choose to be involved or you can leave."

GETTING PEOPLE ON BOARD

The choice to get on board was made very explicit to Marshfield DoorSystems employees at the demarcation event staged by Bill Blankenship and Jerry Mannigel three months into their tenure. Like Harley-Davidson with its slogan "The Eagle Soars Alone," Marshfield DoorSystems also had a slogan for its event: "There's a New Train in Town."

The message was sent at a company-wide meeting staged inside one of the manufacturing plants. People who worked at Marshfield DoorSystems at the time said that they were nervous because there had been a lot of talk going around that something was going to change—it was no secret the company was losing money. When Blankenship and Mannigel called the meetings and made it mandatory for everyone to attend, many assumed the worst. They didn't expect to enter a makeshift hall created inside the plant and decorated as a train station. Railroad-crossing posts—lights and all—flanked either side of the podium where Blankenship stood. An old-fashioned steam-driven passenger train had been printed on a banner and strung up behind him.

People who were there that day said that when Blankenship began to speak his message was clear. "There's a new train in town. You can get on the train or you can choose not to. If you choose not to, when the train leaves the station, you won't be on it."

The train analogy captured people's attention and imagination. Eight years after the ceremony, people still talked about it. The event offered an opportunity for management to communicate a clear message to the entire organization at one time.

One important aspect of the event and the timing is that it coincided with intense outreach from management to the union that represented the hourly workers in the Marshfield DoorSystems manufacturing plants. Broken communications systems at Marshfield DoorSystems had extended to its relationship with the union. It was necessary for the change effort to open the communication lines. Management started by meeting with union representatives and sharing the audited financial statements with them. It was the first time Marshfield DoorSystems management had done that, but it was seen as critical to getting the union "on the train" for change—the union needed to know exactly what was happening with the organization's financials.

Note that Harley-Davidson also initiated closer relations with its union at around the same time it held its York–Milwaukee ride. The purpose is to make sure that the immediate stakeholders—employees, investors, unions—get the same information at the same time.

COMMUNICATION METHODS AS
A MODEL FOR CHANGE

Public commitments to change work best and are most credible when the form they take reinforces the kind of change the company hopes to create. When Howard Schultz said that his employees have his permission to start again if they pull a substandard shot, you believe him, partly because he was willing to lose $6 million in revenue to make sure they all had the skills to do it. He made a commitment to quality, and he gave them permission to do the same.

Carol Bernick's public commitment also promised change by manifesting the kind of change she wanted to see, namely a more open, communicative, collaborative Alberto-Culver. Her goal was "to recruit everyone in the battle and get every single person focused on the same goals. After a long history of management's keeping its cards close to the vest, we needed to open up and explain the business to our people. Once the facts were on the table, we would find the people who were excited about responding to the challenges."

Once she had her Workplace 2000 change coalition in place, as well as a change vision for the GDL program, she held a "state of the company" address. The event was a two-hour, all-company meeting that allowed her to provide an intensive view into the current state of the company as well as her vision of where the company could go.

The event took place in a meeting hall. Before the employees arrived, Carol scattered pennies all over the floor. When they entered the hall, no one picked them up. Later, she asked employees to guess what the pennies were. When no one came up with the answer, she said, "That penny represents our total profit on a bottle of Alberto VO5 shampoo." She then went on to explain where VO5 resided in the firm's overall strategy, and the role that the chain of beauty supply stores called Sally Beauty Supply played as the powerful, growing, profitable driver of the entire Alberto-Culver Company. "The process of turning our employees into businesspeople had begun," Bernick said.

Commenting on the event, one informant said, "The communication change and sharing that information was huge and it was like, 'Holy smokes! We've got a problem here in the United States. We better do something about it.' I think all those things, together, helped turn this thing around."

The pennies story at Alberto-Culver was not only a clarion call to action regarding the financial condition of the Americas Group. It also exemplified the very cultural values and norms that the coalition would be indoctrinating into the rest of the organization. Through it, Alberto-Culver initiated a set of behaviors to focus on intense communication, teamwork, respect for individuals, trust, and the market as the firm's raison d'être.

CHANGE CONFUSION

In the examples from Harley-Davidson, Marshfield DoorSystems, and Alberto-Culver, people who attended the public events demarking change all experienced a level of excitement and faith in the actions of management. The change felt real, and people consistently understood what change meant across the organization.

That experience is not universal. MediaCo, EquipmentCo, BenefitsInc, and Motorola did not have formal demarcation events. Instead, they used traditional internal communication channels to communicate changes that took place as part of the effort, such as leadership changes, brand launches, and program changes. But we have already explained that the communications systems within these firms were largely dysfunctional, with the result that the information came not at once, but in small trickles.

MediaCo seemed to invest the most in communicating its change efforts through existing channels. For example, employees received small, incremental communications regarding the change process in the form of meetings with designated liaisons, and then ongoing write-ups in the company newsletter and posters in hall-ways. But these messages seemed like siloed efforts, according to informants. They did not seem to be part of a coherent plan. One executive manager said, "We seem to change direction every three months, every four months. . . . This is just sixth in a line of six that we've been through. And in six months it'll go away and we'll do something else. . . . I spend . . . an inordinate amount of time talking to my peers about 'Gee, what's the latest rumor? Who's gone next?' or 'When is this big workforce reduction?'"

Such confusion affected the strategies that MediaCo business unit managers used to implement the change process. One of the managers tasked with implementing the overall market-based strategies told us about his approach with his team: "Tell me who I could be today. Don't worry about tomorrow. We'll do that the right way, the long way through all these process steps with the market-segmentation team. But if I could . . . make an impact on the marketplace right away . . . the company's going to go, 'This thing works!' It's about getting wins on the board as soon as possible!"

This manager's approach illustrates how the lack of a strong guiding coalition with a plan for change communicated in a clear, public manner created short-term thinking and a tolerance for inconsistent processes. MediaCo did make further progress in its efforts to become more market-focused, but change was slow and marked by a high level of confusion among MediaCo employees.

EquipmentCo employees experienced a similar level of confusion. EquipmentCo had a relatively new leader, who had been appointed when the executive at the firm's parent company recognized the need for change and initiated the change effort. The new leader, Adam Deutsch, created a change coalition to construct a vision for change. Yet the lack of a clear demarcation event caused employees to speculate whether the ideas espoused by Deutsch were held by all the executives within the company. When another employee, Frank Graves, was promoted to an executive role, an informant said, "He's got a very different view of the industry . . . so it'll be interesting to see how we go down parallel paths. I mean, I could see or sense different messages coming from Adam than were coming from Frank. . . . It may end up being just absolutely fine, but I think everyone is kind of pausing. Like, 'What's going to happen next?'"

And we already discussed how the BenefitsInc brand effort was executed offstage and brought back into the company in a soft manner that was meant to be nonthreatening. There were practical reasons for this approach—the company wanted to accomplish the rebranding within the jurisdiction of the corporate sponsor that had domain over communications. But the result was an expensive program that did not "belong" to anyone inside the company. Thus when the new brand image and related advertising rolled out, there was no unified approach for members of the firm to address the gap between what the market wanted and what the firm could provide. As one informant explained, the leaders "never told the divisions to do anything" different related to the new brand.

The problems these businesses experienced as a result of poor communications were not superficial. On the contrary, the siloed efforts within MediaCo, EquipmentCo, and BenefitsInc, coupled with the lack of communication, bred a great deal of animosity among corporate employees. Nonmarketing personnel did not like or trust the nature of the changes they saw, and a number of people reported that marketing was trying to "dominate other functions in the firm." In these companies there was much more suspicion, resentment, and ambiguity surrounding the kind of changes that were pursued than we saw at Marshfield Door-Systems, Alberto-Culver, and Harley-Davidson.

The suspicion and distrust seemed to relate to the challenge of taking a *marketing*-focused approach to change instead of *market*-focused, as discussed in the previous chapter. The marketing personnel tasked with creating change in the organizations did not have the in-house authority or trust to actually achieve the goals they were given.

Yet it is important to note that many of these companies had the steps right in the abstract—they recognized the need for change, they built a coalition, and they formed a vision. Their challenges arose because neither the coalition itself nor the vision it created had company-wide validation. We saw at Harley-Davidson that employees really felt with the LBO and the York–Milwaukee ride that they were getting their company back. In contrast, no one we spoke to at MediaCo, EquipmentCo, or BenefitsInc communicated a sense of belonging when it came to their companies and the changes they faced. Thus, when it came time to go public, the vision did not have the kind of coherence necessary to galvanize a divided public.

A MIDDLE GROUND: SIGNALING CHANGE

When Chris Galvin was promoted in 1993 to president and chief operating officer of Motorola, it served as a de facto demarcation event. While there was no formal meeting to communicate how things would change, the nature of his appointment sent a clear signal. Chris was a "marketing guy" given one of the top seats in traditionally engineering-driven Motorola. His internal and external statements consistently communicated a vision of creating a more market-focused Motorola.

The first five to seven years of his tenure focused on training executives in market focus. But hiring Mike Zafirovski from GE to be the president of Motorola PCS in 2000 signaled a significant change from the company's historical engineering focus. Within a matter of months Zafirovski was reporting directly to Galvin, and both took an intimate interest in product development and how it was changing to be more focused on what customers would want to buy. Both executives—Galvin and Zafirovski—demonstrated that interest by attending the weekly Motorola PCS product strategy meetings. It was these quiet moves more than a performed, dramatic demarcation event that signaled clearly that change was happening.

In our view, the companies that took a more public stance changed faster, but the countercultural moves in Motorola served a similar purpose with (eventually) similar results to the more dramatic approach of Harley-Davidson, Marshfield DoorSystems, and Alberto-Culver.

CONCLUSION

Demarcation events to communicate change are an important and critical step in the change process. They signal to all employees that the company is making a true and clear commitment to change and that it wants everyone on board. Leaders also get their first chance to model the kind of change they are promoting. Through focused communication, they set the stage to show and promote changes in norms and behaviors that are critical to convert the culture from its siloed and secretive past to a more collaborative and communicative present.

STAGE II

REINVENT

6

WALKING THE TALK

THE TERM "POCKET VETO" HAD BECOME A CONSIS-
tent part of the corporate vernacular at Motorola in the early
2000s. The term referred to the all-too-common practice among
subgroup executives of ignoring a decision or order by a senior
officer in the firm and just going about business as usual. Junior
executives would frequently execute a pocket veto if a higher-level
executive canceled a project that he or she oversaw. In secret, the
junior executive would continue with the project.

Continuing with a project that had been canceled would appear to be difficult, but the way Motorola was organized made
it surprisingly easy. One Motorola senior manager explained the
fiefdom structure that prevailed in the PCS organization before
the era of Mike Zafirovski, which allowed such secret operations to take place: "There is a history of one hundred and forty

different platforms that we have in PCS, because we created that entrepreneurial spirit—but nobody worked together. There's kind of a culture that says that people don't necessarily work together all that effectively, and don't feel like they need to necessarily because in your little sandbox [you're allowed to do what you want]."

Far from criticized, pocket vetoes were heralded in Motorola lore, and the people who issued them were consistently viewed in the ranks as doing the right thing. Pocket veto practitioners played into the widely held belief that senior leaders were out of touch and didn't understand why a project was needed. Pocket veto rebels assumed that once the project had progressed to a certain stage and was beginning to show value, the Motorola superiors would realize their mistake and reward the commitment and audacity of the pocket veto team. In some cases, rewards did accrue, which only reinforced the idea that people could just do what they wanted and could ignore leadership edicts.

WALKING THE TALK: INFLUENTIAL LEADERS NEED TO EMBODY CHANGE

The pocket veto exemplifies the issue of behavior change that many resurgent companies need to confront. After the change coalition has gone public and communicated a vision for change, the real work of creating change from within begins. That requires a new set of behaviors consistent with the culture and values laid out in the vision.

The form used to communicate change to the broader organization can be a helpful tool for modeling the kind of behaviors that the firm sees as essential for its future. Carol Bernick wanted a more communicative Alberto-Culver, for example, so she modeled change by becoming more communicative herself. But even the most high-impact events will leave some skeptics.

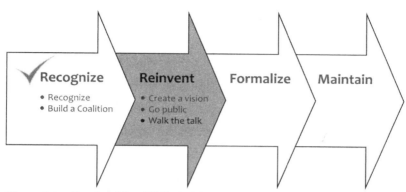

Figure 6-1:   Leaders Must Walk the Talk of Change as Part of Reinvention

To win them over, influential leaders and employees need to begin modeling change through relevant and consistent actions (see Figure 6-1). Change is infectious; it will spread if given the right push. Leaders need to model the kind of change they expect to see, prepare and train organization members in those behaviors, and reinforce the adoption of change with recognition.

For Motorola, that meant deglamorizing the pocket veto and other common practices that celebrated individualism and engineering-centrism, and undermined efforts to create a collaborative and communicative environment. For other companies, it meant doing away with an equivalent practice that bred division and conflict—every company had one.

For example, Marshfield DoorSystems had a tradition on the shop floor of managers issuing "hot lists" that forced shop workers to process their orders first, regardless of which order was officially next in the queue. Leaders would modify the hot list daily. The sales vice president might push up one customer first thing in the morning, but then the manufacturing vice president would reshift the list in order to gain efficiencies and ensure that all the stations in the plant were being used in the best way possible. Then the logistics personnel might modify the list again to ensure that the delivery trucks were full before they pulled out. Hot lists were not an official approach. Officially, the plant had policies in place that determined which orders came first, but privately the leaders were undermining each other.

The conflicting nature of these activities led to confusion and poor allocation of resources, which makes it difficult to impossible to successfully implement any solution. Worse, these underground policies created feelings of distrust and a lowered willingness to communicate openly; at two firms, the situation became so bad that executives reportedly stopped talking to each other.

Conveying the need for collaboration and respect through the ranks of the organization is very difficult if top managers undermine each other. People in power influence those junior to them. That influence can be used to good effect in this early stage of Reinvention. Research has shown that high-status professionals who are viewed as competent and effective can promote desired norms of behavior in others by modeling the same behaviors they want to see.[1] Over time, behaviors breed a shift in culture. For example, leaders who seek more communication and collaboration can engender those behaviors in their employees by being more communicative and collaborative themselves.

Ongoing Communication from the Top

At Marshfield DoorSystems, leaders reinforced and confirmed their commitment to change at the very beginning of the process by instituting quarterly, all-company meetings to communicate plans and actions to hourly workers. One executive told Gary that the guiding philosophy was "We're gonna stop the plant. We're gonna hold meetings of our people every quarter. We're gonna get face-to-face with these people . . . and we're gonna talk about what we're doing, what we're up to, and why we're doing it."

Marshfield DoorSystems was a manufacturing-oriented company; the symbolism of stopping the plant four days a year to inform employees about company actions and to provide a forum for hourly workers to ask questions of management represented a staggering commitment to change. Nonetheless, it took a few meetings for employees to believe that change was real and that the executives were truly walking the talk of change, not just talking about it.

One executive recalled, "The first couple of quarters, we got a lot of rocks thrown at us. The comment I heard was 'When are *they* going to fix it?' And I used to say, 'Who do you think 'they' is? 'They' is us. You're looking at 'em!' . . . By the third or fourth quarter, that went way down. People started to say, 'Gee, we are staying the course on this.'"

Engagement with Senior Managers

In addition to formal meetings to improve communication, high-level managers showed their commitment to change through increased presence in the plants and in the offices where the work was done. Far from locking themselves away on the executive floor, the leaders of successful change efforts made themselves available to people at all levels of the company.

For example, Bill Blankenship of Marshfield DoorSystems spent significant time walking through the plant and talking to the firm's hourly workers. One Marshfield employee recalled how meaningful Blankenship's visits were at the time: "He knew your name! And he might know something about your machine. . . . Somebody mentioned something to him that you used it at one hundred and eighty degrees instead of one hundred and twenty degrees . . . and he gets out there and he goes, 'You still running that at one eighty?' And the people are like, 'How does he know that I just switched to one eighty?' He remembered that stuff and asked the question."

One frontline worker at Marshfield DoorSystems at the time said of Bill Blankenship, "He also showed people he cared. . . . He showed his face in the factory! Came in on all shifts. Knew people's names. He started quarterly meetings. Told us how the mill was running: profits, losses. Started incentives for safety. . . . He started doing these different programs that showed people he did care. He wanted people here. He didn't want people getting hurt. . . . Our business started picking up and we started making money. So people started trusting him."

Marshfield's Jerry Mannigel was also known as someone who would talk to employees. He would jaw with them about their work, or about fishing, hunting, and what was new in the town of Marshfield. Employees were not used to seeing vice presidents walking around the plant, talking to people, addressing their concerns, or asking about their work. Seeing senior management connect with people on a personal level as they echoed their plan and reported on the organization's progress was reassuring. It made people feel involved.

At Harley-Davidson, management actions were equally important to reassure employees of the commitment to change. The thirteen investors started with an advantage—they were much more connected to the business and personally vested in its success than people perceived AMF had been. Through their actions, the thirteen members of the change coalition exemplified many of the core values the firm embraces today.

One informant said, "Vaughn Beals, in my estimation, was the best manager, most intelligent person, I've ever seen in my life. . . . There wasn't a phony bone in his body. If he thought you could do a better job, he wasn't firing for effect. He really thought you could do a better job or do the job in a better way.

And when he was wrong, he'd admit it. I just really have a lot of respect for the guy."

Similarly to the informant from Marshfield DoorSystems, this informant from Harley said how important seeing and engaging with the management team were to his ability to trust in the change. His experience of this connection was very personal. He shared the following anecdote:

> In the height of the financial problems surrounding the corporation, my dad had a heart attack. . . . My mom was going through a tough time, my dad was in the hospital, lot of pressure on me, right? I see Vaughn coming in the hallway and my first reaction was "Oh, shit! What's he gonna say to me now? Now what assignments do I have? Now what do I gotta do?" He stopped me in the hallway and said, "I heard your dad's sick. Take whatever time you need to straighten your family stuff out. Nothing is more important." I never told him my dad was sick. I never said anything to a lot of people here. That was my cross to bear for that year. He found out somehow, someway. He sought me out. He gave me the clarity and that it was okay. And this was the hard-driving, killer, the real archetypical American hard-driving manager . . . and he sought me out to give me his permission to do what I needed to do. I'll never forget that experience. I still, as you can tell, it chokes me up. That was almost twenty years ago.

Symbols of Change

This investment in change showed up as well in a number of symbolic ways within Harley-Davidson in the years following the LBO. The leadership eliminated assigned parking at headquarters; senior executives participated alongside more junior employees in demo rides, HOG rallies (events for the Harley Owners Group), and local rides; the leaders consolidated the cafeterias at headquarters into one facility that everyone could use; and they instituted a policy requiring all Harley-Davidson employees to buy their personal motorbikes through the dealer network, just as any customer would. These efforts served to make Harley-Davidson a more connected place, and gave employees clear opportunities to experience the organization just as a customer would.

But perhaps the most significant and influential action on the part of senior management at the time was to meet with union representatives and open up the Harley-Davidson financial books to them. That had never been done before. One informant said of the decision, "When you know how desperate the situation is and you truly need assistance—whether it's from the salaried workforce or the union workforce or your lending institutions or your dealer network or the government or whomever it may be . . . I think you've got to show them the facts. . . . If you're really in trouble and you need someone to extend a helping hand, whoever that may be, you damn well better be honest with them. The way you're honest with them is opening up the books; and sharing management responsibility; working with the union; looking at the union as a fellow stakeholder."

At Motorola, changes in the way things were done likewise had huge symbolic resonance within the firm. Within the first two years of Mike Zafirovski's tenure, for example, he established an executive review board (ERB) at corporate headquarters. The ERB was responsible for worldwide product planning. It was a large, cross-functional group, with representation across the organization, but *there were only five voting members:* the four regional vice presidents responsible for sales and operations in North America, Latin America, Asia, and EMEA (Europe, the Middle East, and Africa) respectively, and a vice president of product portfolio management as the chair. No product could be added to the portfolio of products in development—and therefore, no product could be funded—unless the five voting ERB members agreed. This was a huge shift at Motorola, where engineering had traditionally prevailed.

"Engineering, non-voting member?" One executive informant said. "I mean, imagine that in Motorola! The engineers don't get to vote on what goes into the portfolio! Huge shift. They're still screaming about it."

TRAINING FOR CHANGE

When senior managers behave in ways and promote policies that are consistent with what they are saying about change, it creates a lot of trust and goodwill within the organization. People see that the change effort is sincere and real.

Employees then need help assimilating and reflecting those behaviors. We have seen that the momentum created by the communications event, and followed up with consistent senior management decisions and actions, can be effectively accelerated and reinforced with the help of formal training programs that provide employees with the skills and processes needed in the new organization. The positive impact we have seen from formal training is consistent with research on organizational cultures, which suggests that organizations that explicitly state their expectations around norms of behavior and values ensure that employees know what to do in given situations.[2] Effective formal training programs are aligned with the processes and approaches outlined in the company's vision for change.

Training played a critical role at Harley-Davidson, for example. As part of its vision for change, Harley-Davidson adopted employee involvement, statistical operator control, and just-in-time inventory programs to deal with quality issues and cash-flow challenges. Harley-Davidson realized it needed these tools when its leaders decided to benchmark its performance against other companies and toured a Honda plant in the United States. While there, Vaughn Beals, Tom Gelb, and others saw that the Japanese achieved 30 percent greater productivity with a fraction of the parts' inventory.[3] One of the outcomes from that visit was that Harley-Davidson made statistical operator control classes required training for every employee.

Although MediaCo and EquipmentCo were not ultimately successful in their overall efforts to realize change, they too instituted organization-wide training programs aimed at changing behaviors within their organizations—and the trainings themselves appeared to be well conceived and organized. In both companies, the training focused on interpersonal problem-solving skills. The purpose of the workshops was twofold: first, they aimed to reinforce organizational values by connecting those values to actual work people did on a day-to-day basis; second, the workshops provided role-play and modeling activities to teach people new cognitive schemas for dealing with situations in ways consistent with the new organizational values.

At MediaCo and EquipmentCo, the training programs began with a discussion of the organizations' new values and how they related to day-to-day responsibilities. The approach used in these workshops was "sell and tell"—the values had already been established by the coalition team, so the workshop activities were geared not toward identifying and developing those values, but rather toward communicating about them, and explaining why they were important. The "sell and tell" method has been shown in certain contexts to create the same level of goal commitment as the participative model.

The act of discussing and recognizing the values *before* training appeared to provide meaning for training participants. They were better able to recognize why the subsequent training modules were important to the organization and its employees, which created a higher level of motivation to participate in the exercises, learn the cognitive tools, and apply them outside the workshop. Although these organizations ultimately did not become market-focused, that failure was due not to lack of training, but rather—as we discuss later in this chapter—in part to lack of cultural agreement at the highest level.

USING REWARDS TO REINFORCE BEHAVIOR

Guiding coalitions used various rewards and recognition tools to encourage and reinforce behaviors that were consistent with the change effort. The most prevalent use of rewards and recognition was interpersonal. It usually came in the form of communications that showed approval or disapproval for particular comments or actions.

As we mentioned in Chapter 4 an important part of the change effort at Marshfield DoorSystems was a revised focus on safety. One member of the Marshfield DoorSystems coalition commented on its recognition program: "We wanted to have some type of incentive, but we didn't want an incentive system that masked problems . . . so we started out with gifty things. . . . For the first few years we handed out coffee mugs, fire alarms, first-aid kits, et cetera. Lots of T-shirts, et cetera—just knickknacks with logos, et cetera. When we hit one million hours [without a work-loss accident], we gave really nice winter jackets for one of the prizes, right before the winter in November, so it was perfect timing! People really wore those with pride! Some still wear them!"

Similar trinkets were used at Harley-Davidson for completing training programs. People also wore T-shirts and other branded clothing from events such as the Eagle Soars Alone ride, demo rides, and rallies.

Of all the participating companies, Alberto-Culver most actively used rewards and recognition to build momentum for cultural change. Alberto-Culver focused mainly on positive reinforcement. As we explained in Chapter 4, Alberto-Culver's efforts to change the culture of the organization focused on the use of the Growth Development Leader (GDL) program. Alberto-Culver made sure that there were no negative consequences for people who weren't chosen as a GDL. Those who were chosen, however, were subject to ongoing accountability. There were formal evaluations put in place that allowed employees to evaluate their GDLs in the same way they would evaluate their business unit managers (recall that the GDL was often not a person's direct boss).

As one informant said of the impact, "The people in your GDL group are evaluating you every year. . . . It is not published, but it's very public. . . . Everybody goes into a room and the awards start getting handed out. The guys who are glued to their chairs and never getting up and getting an award with red faces are very, very identifiable. Then those that need a wheelbarrow to take all the awards back to their office are also very visible. So there is a separation between the haves and the have-nots. It is a very, very public thing. Because of the openness of it, you go back to your group and say, 'Thank you very much. I'm glad you appreciate the job I'm doing' or 'I'm sorry I've been such a knucklehead for this past year.'"

INAUTHENTICITY: WHEN LEADERS SAY ONE THING AND DO ANOTHER

So far in this chapter we have focused on the positive actions that promote and accelerate change. But change can also be halted— even stopped in its tracks. One of the fastest ways for leaders to do that is to behave in ways that are inconsistent with the stated goals

for change. When leaders do not follow through on their promises; when they say one thing but do another; when they promote
communication but then keep secrets or obfuscate in their own
communication—it kills any commitment that in-house personnel have in the resurgence effort.

Such inconsistency was, sadly, a common experience at
MediaCo. One telling example was layoffs. When the change efforts started, top management had made clear their intention to
reduce the number of executives. But everyone was sent to behavior training with Senn-Delaney, and months after training the
reductions still had not happened.

Commenting on the experience, one participant said, "I think
there's this big disconnect. You have those things, the values and
visions of the company from Bob's mouth. But that's about as far
as they fall. . . . I mean, it's kind of tough not to talk about that
when . . . we know as a company that we're thirty to forty percent
cost disadvantaged versus our major competitors . . . in terms of
vice presidents or officer level leadership. . . . So if we figure there
are two hundred officers in the company . . . that means there are
sixty too many. So we've gone through about this six-to-nine-
month period of everybody waiting for this shoe to drop to get
rid of sixty people. I don't know if they understand how stifling
that is. . . . I think people would be much more understanding and
appreciative and energized for better or for worse around, 'Hey,
we've got sixty too many officers. We've got to figure it out, okay?
And we're going to do something about it.' Instead of month after
month, after month, after month of culture transformation exercises. Because people say, 'Wait a minute! This doesn't sync up!
You tell me one thing but you're doing another.'"

Ironically, the cultural training in which people at MediaCo
participated may have made the importance of management actions even more salient. The Senn-Delaney training included a

module on the shadow of the leader, in which participants were sensitized to the fact that employees interpret what is important and appropriate based on the actions of those above them.

Employees saw a lot of people—senior leaders included—giving lip service to change without actually changing. One senior MediaCo executive who asked that his comments not be quoted directly said that it would have been political suicide to say anything negative about the change effort because Bob Smith had invested a lot of personal capital in it, and the company had invested a lot of money. The company aligned incentives with the change program at this early stage, so to get bonuses people had to play along, regardless of how they felt personally.

Another MediaCo senior executive concurred with this view, saying, "It would be *unwise* now if you were in a visible position, not to act in [ways consistent with the change effort], whether you believe it or not. . . . [But] people's actions haven't had to change yet. Their *support*—they've had to *support* what we're doing—but their actions haven't had to change . . . [in terms of] how we do business."

Employees and leaders at EquipmentCo expressed similar frustrations regarding the mixed signals between stated values, training, and the actions required by people up and down the organization. During a visit to the company, Gary had witnessed severe animosity in an exchange between members of the sales department and members of marketing and asked one of his informants about it. The informant replied, "Oh! Totally! . . . There's no love lost between the sales and marketing groups. . . . I would say on the surface, as far as relationships go, things are much better. But I think behind the scenes it's no different. . . . I believe they've been told to play nice. And now they're playing nice."

This same informant said later in that same conversation, "Culture depends on what you see from the top. Part of the training is empowering people and trusting people to make the right decisions, stay true to the brand. But regarding many activities, the president, the vice presidents of EquipmentCo, and occasionally even the CEO of HoldingsInc require their personal sign-off. That, to me, is not consistent with the culture that we're trying to create here."

The divisiveness at EquipmentCo was not limited to cross-functional conflicts. In fact, Gary got a glimpse through his interviews of active dissent from a top manager whose views on the company and what it should be doing were in stark opposition to the philosophy of the change leader. In one typical comment, this dissenter, who was a vice president of sales, said, "This company thinks that developing a plan for promotional activity for the next twelve months is a big deal. It is a big deal if you've never planned before. But let's talk about what we're going to do in the next thirty days, sixty days, ninety days to effect change in the income statement related to the way we sell and what we sell. We're not quite there yet. The point is that I think that we're thinking by putting a plan together, that's a good thing and that's going to generate something positive. That's what they're thinking. A plan is a good thing."

Gary then asked directly about what this sales VP did, especially in public forums, given his disagreement. "I'm on a different path than some of these guys over here," he said. "I'll be honest with you. I'm not with these guys." When Gary specifically asked about the change leader, Adam Deutsch, the speaker said, "And I have a different path than him. I don't think like he does."

This executive eventually left EquipmentCo and bought a reseller business, but he was a high-profile person in the company acting in dismissive ways in private conversations for long enough to form cracks in the change effort. He alone was not responsible for EquipmentCo's failure to change, but he, and others like him, contributed to an erosion of the solidarity necessary for change.

When the Public Image Clashes with Change Goals

The experiences of employees and leaders at MediaCo and Equip-mentCo make clear how demoralizing and divisive it can be to hear leadership making statements that clearly contradict their actions and vice versa, both public and private. This type of con-tradiction is all too frequent in struggling firms. In Chapter 4 we mentioned the struggles of Avon and former CEO Andrea Jung's flawed vision for the iconic beauty company. One element that has contributed to Avon's slide is the inconsistent messages—both explicit and implicit—communicated by Jung to the organization and the world.

The power of the implicit cannot be underestimated in this case. Jung is known for her youth and glamour—it is the rare Jung profile that doesn't note the color of her lipstick or the brand of her shoes. This is admittedly unfair and sexist. Jung is not the first or the only woman executive to dress stylishly, and journalists don't usually mention the attire of, say, Alan Ennis, CEO of Revlon. But the reality is that people—especially public figures—project a message about themselves and their values with their appearance, and Andrea Jung is more Coco Chanel than Tupperware. She has a public, high-profile, executive glamour that has little in common with the real Avon Ladies, who tend to be micro- or small, inde-pendent entrepreneurs still selling products door-to-door in small geographic areas. Avon's "market" in a real way is not the end user of the product but the enormous direct distribution channel, those six million women who are investing their entrepreneurial capa-bilities in selling the promise of youth and beauty to women in their communities. With her conspicuous personal preference for brands like Chanel and Blahnik, Andrea Jung said very clearly she wasn't a member of the team of women she was tasked with representing.

That would be enough to generate a disconnect between public statements and private actions, but Jung further alienated the Avon Ladies by pursuing a retail strategy in the United States with partners like Sears and JCPenney, which would allow Avon enthusiasts to stock up on Skin So Soft and Avon lipsticks while bypassing the local businesswomen who have buoyed the company since its inception.

The US operations for Avon are the company's largest market, but the one that was growing the slowest. Given that lagging status, it might be understandable if Avon were focusing its attentions elsewhere. But Brazil, one of Avon's fastest-growing markets, was also a victim of conflict between public statements and behind-the-scenes action. Here Jung invested in wooing Brazilian Avon Ladies to sell the products, but failed to invest in the infrastructure and processes necessary to support the direct sales force. As a result, fulfillment in Brazil suffered a serious logjam. Inventory management was abysmal. Orders were delayed or lost altogether. The company may have suffered little ill effect if it had had a loyal public and limited competition, but Avon was growing in Brazil precisely because of a lively market for beauty products within a growing economy. Its products appear next to a number of hugely popular beauty brands, most notably Natura, a direct sales beauty company founded by a native Brazilian.[4]

The popularity and home-field advantage of Brazilian companies like Natura make Avon's infrastructure gaffe all the more egregious, because Brazilian Avon Ladies don't sell for one company exclusively. They also sell for other direct product companies. A savvy micro-entrepreneur needs to lose only one sale due to incompetent fulfillment before she stops pushing the product altogether. Sure, she'll sell to a loyalist, but she's not going to work as hard to introduce the product to new customers.

The market issued its judgment on Jung's leadership. Sales fell, and in early 2012 Jung was ousted. The only question is why it took more than twelve years and significant losses to see that her words and her actions did not match.

GETTING THE HANG OF IT:
LEARNING TO MODEL CHANGE

Ideally, leaders should be consistent from the beginning. But in some organizations leaders need to adapt and adjust their behavior to be consistent with the new values of the resurgent firm. MediaCo suffered from some inconsistency between what leaders said were the values of the firm and how people acted in practice. But to their credit, many members of the leadership, including Bob Smith, were working to be consistent with the collaborative, respectful, customer-first environment they claimed to want.

Gary had the privilege of attending the monthly, web-based, all-company conference calls that MediaCo instituted as part of its resurgence, and through that forum he had the opportunity to watch the leaders as they adapted to change. Every meeting included progress on organizational change efforts, along with rotating discussions of various initiatives led by the manager in charge of the effort. Month by month, the president, who reported to Bob Smith, was able to emulate the desired values of the firm more consistently. The impact of his actions on the behavior of others was apparent. For example, during the second or third meeting Gary attended, the president had to twice correct the third-party facilitator for addressing the meetings incorrectly. "This isn't my meeting," he said. "This is our meeting."

In addition, he began including in the agenda a question-and-answer session, and actively solicited post-meeting feedback. This information didn't disappear, as it might at some companies. Instead, the president addressed issues that had arisen at the beginning of the following meeting, and he encouraged people to speak and share. He used code phrases such as "be here now" to remind people of their importance.

Perhaps the most fascinating aspect of his changed behavior was the way he modeled the aspects of respect and appreciation—but with accountability—such that later meetings seemed almost cultlike in their tone. MediaCo did not successfully become a market-focused firm, but a combination of training and consistent modeling of collaborative and inclusive actions by senior management appeared to move the company along on the spectrum toward market focus.

CONCLUSION

Companies aiming to become more market-focused move along on that path when senior leaders—especially members of the change coalition—begin manifesting change through their actions. In short, they walk the talk. Seeing change through the actions of leaders is critical for building trust throughout the organization that the change is real. The organizations that we saw successfully reinvent themselves put in the effort to establish open communication channels within the organization. Effective change leaders were present and engaged with employees at all levels. They did away with symbols of division or hierarchy—such as executive parking spaces, or separate, more elegant office suites. They talked about teamwork and collaboration, and they started by being more team-oriented and collaborative themselves.

In contrast, the transition to a market focus can be threatened when leaders publicly support change while privately engaging in "business as usual." When change leaders do not follow through on commitments or change their ways of doing business, they send the message that the change is not real and that no one has to commit anything to the effort.

A foundation of changed behaviors puts the company on solid ground to move to the next step of the Reinvent stage of market-focused change. The time has come when companies that really want to become more market-focused must reconnect with the customer.

REINVENT

7

DEAR CUSTOMER

Reconnecting with the Market

BY THE TIME THAT THE MARSHFIELD DOORSYSTEMS "New Train in Town" event took place, it was clear that there were deep inconsistencies in the organization's understanding of who the customer was and what the customer wanted. It was no secret to anyone that Marshfield was losing money and market share. Lead times were expanding. The custom manufacturing process had become extremely complicated, which led to manufacturing times as long as twenty-six weeks for a door that could be made with just five hours of labor. Less than half of orders shipped on time during the busy season. Work-in-process was bloated. Quality was horrible, with 10 percent of doors needing to be re-veneered before they left the factory, and continued high field claims for faulty doors.

No one was ignoring these issues, but the solutions were all based on functional or individual views of the problem and different views of the market. Managers and employees often referred to distributors as customers. Sales maintained a hot list of priority orders, but it changed often, creating a lot of confusion and ambiguity. The 1993 strategic plan suggested implementing the Malcolm Baldrige National Quality Benchmark System. But since the firm could not define "quality," shop floor workers used their own definitions, often emphasizing the natural beauty of the wood materials and the artisanship of door construction.

One guiding coalition member said, "You could just tell it by the intensity and perfection that was being put into the doors and the time and the lack of concern about anything but making the door perfect. . . . When I talked to people, we had a cultural focus on making the best door out there. And people were very proud of that. I like to say that it was kinda like the [Paul Masson wine] ad, you know, 'We will sell no wine before its time.' I used to say, 'No door will leave this plant before its time.'"

If Marshfield DoorSystems was to succeed in its efforts to engineer a resurgence, it would need to develop a consistent, shared understanding of the customer and the value proposition of the firm—it needed to know what the *market* wanted and expected from it.

To get there, Bill Blankenship and Jerry Mannigel initiated a program to send employee teams on field visits to customers, distributors, and architects. A group of senior and middle managers met and identified what they believed the firm's value proposition to be, and they developed a questionnaire to serve as a script for the visits to test those ideas.

The questions included, What product features or considerations factor most in your client's selection of wood doors? How do you and your customers define product "quality" in general?

Specific to wood doors on your projects? How do Weyerhaeuser Doors compare to the competition? The team met with all members of the value chain—customers, distributors, architects, and contractors—across a variety of markets over six months in 1994.

The findings from those visits were shocking to many who participated in them. A number of closely held beliefs about the value Marshfield delivered and the value its customers saw were simply wrong. "We were about 180 degrees off," one participant said.

For instance, the Marshfield managers identified durability of the doors as an issue that was important to the contractors and end-use customers they served. When they visited those customers, they confirmed that the view in the market was that Marshfield's doors *were* the most durable . . . but everyone else's doors were good enough.

The same inconsistency arose around Marshfield's internal definition of quality and the expectations of the market. "Uniform and consistent in appearance," one participant said. "We must have heard that a hundred times before it sunk in." Marshfield Door-Systems makes wood doors, so by definition the look and feel of the materials vary, sometimes dramatically, even if the grade of wood is the same. The insight for Marshfield was that architects and builders "want the beauty of wood and the variation—but they want the variation to be narrow." This was in opposition to internal practice on the factory floor, where shop workers focused more on the individual beauty of the particular wood used on one door, not on the consistency across an order. One participant summarized the issue for the company: "One of the biggest things you have to remember in value propositions is what your customer said. Don't reinterpret and change their words into your words. They didn't say 'highest quality.' They said 'uniform and consistent in appearance.'"

RECONNECTING WITH CUSTOMERS

Like Marshfield DoorSystems, firms embarking on change see some progress from the steps outlined in the early chapters of this book. They recognize the need for change, create a change coalition, craft a vision for change, communicate that vision across the organization, and put in place the foundations of a market-focused culture and encourage behaviors that are consistent with the values and actions laid out in the vision. Yet all that work and commitment are not enough. Why? Because the meetings and communication required to identify a vision for change, communicate that vision, and prepare team members to act according to that vision often reveal, if it wasn't clear before, that the business does not really know for sure what the market wants. In the absence of a clear message derived from direct contact with the market, struggling companies often find that employees and stakeholders have and act on different ideas about the customer.

Within the same firm, people may differ in their identification of who the customer is; they may describe what the customer values in dramatically different terms; and they may interpret what the customer needs differently from their peers. Even if there is internal agreement on these matters, that in-house vision may stand in stark contrast to what the market truly wants, needs, or is prepared to embrace. Such inconsistency makes it very difficult for an organization to make progress. For true resurgence, companies need a *Shared Market Understanding*, and a shared commitment to what the company has to offer. This understanding can come only by reconnecting formally and broadly with the market (see Figure 7-1).

The words "formally" and "broadly" are key to defining the kind of outreach that is most effective at this stage. Companies in the midst of change have likely engaged in at least some outreach

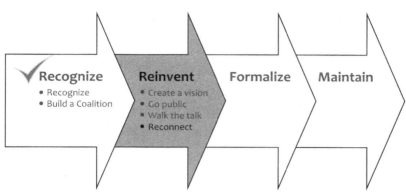

Figure 7-1:   Reconnecting with Customers Is Key to Reinvention

to the market. That outreach may be highly centralized, usually involving senior coalition members reaching out to personal connections or to trusted customers for one-on-one feedback. Senior leaders may have gone on site visits to retailers to see how customers interact with products on the market, or otherwise experience the product through the eyes of the customer. Starbucks CEO Howard Schultz prides himself on visiting Starbucks outlets wherever he travels, and it was the habit of such visits that gave him the firsthand experience needed to see the challenges facing the firm when it embarked on change in early 2008.

Alternatively, companies may have a market-research practice or other functional department whose responsibility is to do research and field visits to identify market practices and latent needs. These sources of market insight are important and necessary in the early stages. These insights often inform the change coalition as it develops the vision for change and communicates it broadly across the business. But that centralized, leadership-centric or research-centric understanding of the market is not enough to galvanize a workforce and create a shared, company-wide understanding of the market and its needs. There is a huge difference for mid-level or frontline employees between hearing a market need expressed from the viewpoint of the CEO and hearing it directly from the customer—that difference is especially large for union workers in companies with contentious management–union relations.

Nor can market research fill in the blanks through formal, qualitative, or quantitative methods. The reasons vary, depending on the firm. Companies that view "market research" as a distinct, almost tribal faction are going to dismiss relevant findings as unimportant. At Motorola, certainly, "research" was demonized as irrelevant to dominant engineering. When Steve Jobs came back into power at Apple in 1997, he fired all the market researchers; the Jobsian view (held by quite a few executives in highly innovative sectors) is that research captures only what customers are doing today, not what they will embrace tomorrow.

Even within organizations where research is an accepted or respected practice, market insights may be meaningless because there is no shared understanding of how to interpret them. Data can be very difficult to interpret without context. Companies that have inconsistent, or frankly wrong, views of who the customer is and what he or she wants are going to either gather the wrong data or draw incorrect conclusions from the data they have. Creating company-wide momentum for change requires that employees hear those needs and wants directly from the customer in a way that creates cross-organizational resonance.

We said in the introduction to this book that the order in which actions are taken is as important as the actions themselves. When it comes to engaging in broad outreach to the market, timing is crucial. Too early and you have not generated the trust and goodwill in your employees that come from investments in improved communication, customer-centric processes, and other cultural advances. Too late and you progress too far with a false or inconsistent view of who the customer is and what he or she wants.

For these reasons, market connection happens best in this interim period—after the company has put in place some cultural and behavioral changes together with a blueprint of processes needed in a market-oriented business, but before setting concrete performance goals.

BROAD CONNECTION WITH THE MARKET

Marshfield DoorSystems took the most formal, hands-on approach toward market connection of all the companies we spent time with. Bill Blankenship, Jerry Mannigel, and the rest of the change coalition of Marshfield DoorSystems planned site visits with employees across their supply chain. As part of that process, they thought a lot about who should visit the customer if those visits were to contribute to a consistent, company-wide understanding of the market.

One guiding coalition member said, "We spent the better part of 1994 with interview teams going out and talking to architects, distributors, and a few general contractors. They were cross-functional teams . . . typically always one sales and marketing person, then there would be one person from manufacturing, generally one person from the quality group, and then at least one person from what we call support services. . . . It's amazing how you can ask one question and three different people can hear three different answers."

Union members were given an opportunity to go on site visits. Marshfield DoorSystems, like many manufacturers, had contentious corporate–union relationships before its transformation. Involving union members in the customer-outreach process was crucial to their efforts to create a Shared Market Understanding in which everyone felt invested.

The same coalition member recalled, "About the union–management thing? We said, 'We need to get rid of that. We need to start working as a team!' So all these cross-functional teams we sent out? We had shop floor people on them too—union president and chief steward. We said, 'This isn't management that wants you to do this, this is the customer who signs all of our paychecks.'"

Allowing representatives from different functions in the firm to attend site visits gave people across the organization an opportunity to hear firsthand what the customer had to say about what they wanted and what they were not happy about. "The key is to have the customer tell you what they want and have the answer interpreted from a manufacturing person's eyes and them saying, 'Yeah, this makes sense.'"

Sharing Findings Broadly in the Organization

Marshfield DoorSystems did not stop with site visits. After each interview, the site visit teams would summarize their findings, which required each team to reach agreement on what they had heard. The visits, together with the process they used to rationalize their findings, created an epiphany for almost everyone. One of the most powerful results was a much deeper understanding of the Marshfield DoorSystems value chain.

We mentioned before that Marshfield employees frequently referred to distributors as "customers," but that was an inaccurate view. In reality, the distributors were not the key users. The key users were the building contractors who bought from those distributors. Contractors were heavily influenced by architects who designed the specs for the doors, at the same time that they needed new ways to appeal to the tenants—the people who had to use and look at those doors every day.

The customer-outreach work helped Marshfield Door-Systems develop a new understanding of its market segments and of the different stakeholders in the door purchase process. One of the main outcomes was a clearer understanding of the different needs contractors had for new construction projects versus tenant improvement, remodels, and renovations. The first type of project segment had longer lead times; the second had four- to six-week lead times, but needed clear commitments on when the doors would arrive. Especially in big cities, where most remodels are in high-rise buildings, the delivery needs to take place at a fixed date and time so that the contractor can reserve the service elevator and put on the pads to protect the walls. If Marshfield missed its delivery window, it might be another week before the contractor could get access again.

One informant explained, "[Building owners] are telling [potential leasers] they can design/decorate the space how they want it, including what kind of doors they want. So after they sign the lease they can move in thirty to sixty days later. So they need those doors fast. For remodel and renovate it is often thirty days." Before Marshfield engaged in its outreach effort, its ever-changing "hot list" made such firm delivery difficult.

The Marshfield change coalition collected the findings from the individual field visits and started to think through the prior assumptions it had about the firm's value proposition. Before the site visits, the implied value proposition at Marshfield was: "We deliver the most durable doors, with the most features and options available, at competitive prices." After the visits it was clear that proposition would not satisfy customers. As one of the change coalition members noted, "That, basically, is a recipe for disaster. Because what you said is, 'We will put more engineering into these doors than anyone else; put more products into these doors; have higher performance criteria [than competitors]; have more features and options than anyone else; and sell them at the lowest price out there. . . .' You can't make money doing that."

Taking what the project team had learned in the field, Marshfield DoorSystems created a new explicit value proposition for the company that said, "Marshfield DoorSystems, Inc.: We supply doors and accessories to our customers that are: uniform and consistent in appearance, 'hassle-free,' delivered on specified dates and times, for a premium price."

To make the value proposition meaningful, the change coalition again had to invest in organization-wide communication, which it did through the company-wide town hall meetings it had been holding every quarter (as discussed in Chapter 5). Presenters included the two union representatives who attended the customer visits. Their presence added an important degree of credibility to the results, since they had heard firsthand what the customers said and they could communicate that message back to their colleagues with the authority that it came from the market.

MARKET OUTREACH AT HARLEY-DAVIDSON

A large number of employees at Harley-Davidson had the opportunity to hear from customers. But unlike the Marshfield DoorSystems approach, which was intentional and designed, the range of employees who participated in the outreach program was a function of the firm's troubled status.

In the early years of Harley-Davidson's resurgence, the firm developed an unconventional marketing program: demo rides. This program was developed largely out of desperation, frugality, and happenstance.

Demo rides were conceived as Harley-Davidson-sponsored events where current and potential customers could test ride the company's motorcycles. Today, they are a hallmark of Harley-Davidson's culture. Demo rides are held at all major motorcycle events, such as Daytona Bike Week and the Sturgis rally, along with regional events coordinated with dealers. But before 1983, demo rides were unheard-of.

As one change coalition member recalled, the demo rides came about as a way to change the poor-quality reputation that Harley had developed before and during the AMF era. He explained, "In the late seventies and early eighties, as bad as things were you could walk into a Harley-Davidson dealership and if you wanted to buy a motorcycle that was fine. But you couldn't sit on it and you couldn't drive it. I'm telling you the truth. You couldn't sit on it because the dealer was afraid the paint job was gonna get scratched from someone's belt buckle or something on their shoe or whatever, and you couldn't ride the motorcycle."

After the LBO Harley-Davidson clearly needed a credibility boost. A few Harley-Davidson employees hit on the idea of demo rides as a way to build that credibility. People from corporate would coordinate with dealers to put on events to give current and prospective riders a chance to test ride the company's new motorcycles. The proposed program was fairly sophisticated, including professional sales training for dealerships, and suggestions to ensure that salespeople met with potential customers after test rides to close deals.

Demo rides were not originally designed to allow large numbers of Harley-Davidson employees to engage with customers. On the contrary, then (as now) the demo rides were organized by a small group of full-time people who handled logistics. But that small team was not large enough to staff the events, and Harley-Davidson didn't have the money to hire or rent event staff. For the demo rides to work, Harley-Davidson employees from other functions needed to volunteer.

Even with such ad hoc staffing, the cost of the program in the first year Harley ran it was $3 million. "Vaughn kept saying, 'How many more motorcycles are we going to sell? Where's the payback?'" one informant said. Eventually, the investors agreed to test the program. Three initial demo rides drew huge crowds, and management was satisfied that the payback in new sales was worthwhile.

As important as new sales were, the demo rides brought something unanticipated and even more important in the long term: a Shared Market Understanding. Vaughn Beals attended some of the first demo rides because he was skeptical that they would bring any benefit, and worried about how they would run. One engineer who participated in one of the first demo rides recalled, "We would work during the day and then we'd go back to the hotel in the evening and talk. Vaughn would buy dinner and we'd all talk about how it went. You know, 'Is it going okay? Should we do something different? What did we learn?'"

Beals's presence and those spontaneous evening meetings turned what started as informal sharing into a formal data-gathering session that codified, and later formalized, the lessons from the market.

In the beginning, the demo rides had mostly sales and marketing volunteers, as well as some senior executives and engineers. Very soon, however, employees from all over the company began to staff them, and those employees all began to see the customer have the same problems and experience the same pleasures from the bikes. The Shared Market Understanding that everyone developed as a result of their participation was not part of the original plan, but once the effects became apparent Harley-Davidson institutionalized the concept.

One change coalition member said, "What came out of all of this was the exact perfect mix, where you're getting a guy in manufacturing, a guy in engineering, and a guy in sales all working the same event on the weekend, and seeing the customer experience the same problem. And the three of you sitting down for a beer afterwards and saying, 'Hey, did you see that shitty paint job? Did you hear the guy comment on it?' And the production guy saying, 'You know if we just polish that a little better that wouldn't happen.' And the engineering guy saying, 'Maybe if we bent that metal different, it'd be easier to polish.' It was just more meaningful, because you saw a customer experience that problem. You know, you saw it firsthand and you wanted to solve it!"

Almost everyone we spoke to had a similar story of how the demo rides transformed the way they thought about and understood the customer. Another informant who was a director at Harley-Davidson said, "It gave us a sense of urgency that quality was bad, because you heard it. . . . The low-rider—a great new product we had just come out with—leaks like a sieve. . . . We heard all those things. . . . We heard the horror stories. We heard the frustrations of customers. So even if you weren't on the manufacturing line, you quickly lost this feeling that 'Hey, we're great and you ought to love us anyway.' You knew that there were problems and we had to work on it quickly. So it makes the problem real to all of us. . . . It gave us a greater sense of urgency to get out to the customers and bring something back to our own jobs. Even when I go to rallies now . . . I come back with a greater sense of contribution to the business, visioning, and focus than I had before."

Direct contact with customers did not replace other ways of gaining customer insights. Market research remained an important way that Harley-Davidson gathered insights about its market. But direct customer contact helped Harley-Davidson employees to *interpret* those market insights and translate them into real actions that the company could take. "Many other companies, I think . . . run the real risk of what I call 'antiseptic research,'" said an employee from Harley-Davidson's market-research arm. "What happens is they get the data . . . and that's the customer to them, that three-ring binder or that data set. That ain't the customer, you know? It may help you understand who they are and what they want and what they need—*but it ain't the customer.* The customer's a person. . . . You don't put tattoos on statistics—you put tattoos on people. You have parties for people, [not for] statistics. . . . You obviously can't—when you sell one hundred and seventy-five thousand units a year—you can't go out and you can't shake everybody's hand, spend the night drinking beer with them, and those other kinds of things. You can't do that. But at least you can do it with enough people that you do recognize that there are people behind those statistics."

Though it wasn't scripted or planned, the entire process of getting employees out into the field had similar effects at Harley-Davidson as at Marshfield DoorSystems. Harley-Davidson did not follow up those demo rides by creating formal "value proposition" definitions as Marshfield did, but the Harley team members nonetheless developed a Shared Market Understanding, which gave terms such as "Harley riders" and "sport bike riders" clear meaning to everyone, and allowed employees to develop clear ideas of market segments and target customers.

ALTERNATIVE WAYS OF BUILDING CONNECTIONS

It is not feasible in many organizations to give a large number of employees an opportunity to go on a site visit like the ones organized formally by Marshfield DoorSystems and serendipitously by Harley-Davidson. But resurgent firms must somehow reconnect with the market and with their customers. They must develop a Shared Market Understanding and bring a representative set of customer stories and experiences back to share across the organization. These actions are absolutely critical if companies want to capitalize on the internal changes around culture. Ideally, that reconnection must resonate with and have a real effect on employees across the organization—from marketing and sales, as well as manufacturing and other operational functions. It should also go deep so that the people doing the work that most directly affects the customer have an interest in that customer's happiness.

Motorola was unable to send a representative percentage of its employees into the market to gather insights from the customer for practical reasons. The PCS division had more than ten thousand employees, which made broad outreach difficult. Another challenge comes from the nature of the product. PCS had corporate clients, but the end users were consumers whose usage patterns varied widely.

Nonetheless, Motorola's commitment to becoming more market- and customer-focused, working from a coherent view of that market, was sincere and deep. One long-term employee said about that commitment, "[Mike Zafirovski] came in hitting the ground running. Very customer focused and impressed the hell out of a lot of us. . . . He continued to drive to listen to the customer. He was very customer oriented. He loves to go talk and see customers."

As discussed in previous chapters, Motorola made investments in the firm's culture so that the customer orientation could come through. At this stage in its resurgence, employees could feel the difference. As one change coalition member said, "One of the tenets of culture that I do see is about breaking boundaries down, making sure nobody ever feels more special than somebody else. It's a notion that it's not about power, but being about shared vision . . . being a generally collaborative process."

Motorola worked to emphasize and integrate the needs of the customer through changes in process. In Chapter 6 we highlighted the product development and product review processes that Motorola implemented as part of its efforts to create change. The Executive Review Board (ERB), as mentioned, was populated by team members across the divisions, but voting rights were given only to the regional market heads. This decision put the customer very much at the center of the product development process because the leaders responsible for building business and delivering product in specific geographic markets had the ultimate say about what would meet the needs of their audience.

Motorola complemented these process changes with a number of research and fieldwork programs aimed at gathering customer insights, conducting consumer research, and bringing personal stories back to share in the organization.

For example, one program involved focused fieldwork, the aim of which was to uncover customer needs and trends and communicate those findings to the relevant groups within Motorola. The fieldwork program was led by the Global Design Planning (GDP) team, which used qualitative research methods to understand customer usage patterns and future needs. These field visits were highly focused and very narrow in terms of the number of people who went—field visits were led by market research, not by a cross-functional team the way they were at Marshfield DoorSystems. But the research team knew they had a broad audience for their findings, so they brought a video camera with them so they could bring back relevant videography to share with different business units. A broad number of employees were not able to go into the field themselves, but they still heard the key messages from the field through the video stories captured by the field team and translated for use through the broader organization.

In addition to the field visits, Motorola created and invested authority in a consumer insight group. Using qualitative methods, that group did research on customers across Motorola's markets, and from that work it was able to create a framework that applied to customers across all global markets: communication; business use; social use; and price (entry level to premium/ exclusive). Within this basic framework fit five customer-use profiles: everyday communication; easy business; corporate business; networked entertainment; and personal style. This consumer insight framework came up in almost every conversation Gary had at Motorola PCS. People referred to it; while telling stories they often elaborated on different segments. Motorola began defining its products in relation to the framework first, and discussing specific product functions second—a marked contrast to the more ad hoc, engineering-focused method used prior to the transformation. This framework enabled Motorola employees to discuss various handset and service initiatives with a common, market-driven understanding of what it was trying to accomplish.

Alone, research gathering would not have done much for Motorola, largely because of the long-held antagonism that we have already highlighted between the marketing and engineering departments. Research was considered a product of marketing and therefore was suspicious. But matched with the process- and culture-oriented changes, Motorola's efforts to develop a deeper understanding of the customer gained more traction.

CONNECTING EMPLOYEE ACTIONS
TO MARKET OUTCOMES

Participants at Marshfield DoorSystems and Harley-Davidson explicitly described the way that seeing the customer experience a problem made that problem real and created a sense of commitment to solve it. In other words, field visits give employees the ability to see in concrete ways how the work that they do on a daily basis affects the customer.

As we've said, not every company can find a way to give employees that direct experience. But creating that connection between the work done and the impact on the customer seems to be core to all these customer-outreach experiences.

Alberto-Culver did not initiate a broad and deep program of field visits. But it did look for ways to better capitalize and sell through its channels, improve its market insights, and connect employee work to customer outcomes.

The effort to better define and use channels began in the mid-1990s and accelerated in the late 1990s when Alberto-Culver hired a number of outside executives with industry experience. Unlike the new hires at BenefitsInc and Motorola, these professionals were integrated into the organization and helped define and create a shared understanding of Alberto-Culver's channels so the business could more effectively capitalize on them.

As one informant noted, "Those guys have really driven the business to a new level . . . not from necessarily all new products, but a lot of our growth has been capturing distribution we didn't have. By hiring the teams that . . . knew the [channel] inside and out—maybe lived in that market, knew the category, and could sell people on the Alberto-Culver franchise."

Alberto-Culver fortified this work to optimize channel sales with some focused field visits to learn how customers view and use the company's products. The company had hired a number of experienced senior marketing people when Carol first stepped into her leadership role, and with their guidance the firm began using different, field-based techniques for developing a better understanding of the end user—the consumer—and what they looked for in the products they buy. One informant from the finance department said, "We've only recently stepped up and are doing [market research] so that we really get into [understanding consumer needs]. . . ."

One Alberto-Culver marketing executive led an effort to do field research in the homes of end users to understand the impulses to buy, use, and discard beauty products. The finance informant said of him, "He's actually in women's bathrooms . . . trying to get an understanding of what they have in skin care, how they use lotions, how they use facial care products, and everything like that. 'What do they do? What do they do in their bathroom?' . . . They were just filming women in their houses explaining what's going on in their bathrooms to a little guy with a mustache. It's really funny seeing this little guy in a mustache hiding out in a closet while this lady is in her bathroom explaining that she uses this body wash or that lotion and it's to get rid of the wrinkles around her eyes."

Another senior marketing executive said, "We did enough in-homes to get some understanding of the fundamentals of the categories we compete in, in terms of behavior, storage, consumption. . . . How does a body wash get [stored and forgotten] underneath the cabinet in the bathroom? Well, it came from the grocery store at some point, but how did it cycle through the shower and then lost its presence in the shower to become a residual product that never gets consumed? How does something become dormant? . . . Those are important questions if you really want to follow the behavior of what goes on. Why is there, in any home that I've been into and I have yet to see one where there is not one brand of body wash or fragrance? There's two, three, four, five. . . . So seeing that behavior in homes and seeing consumers use it helps you understand those kinds of things. What's convenient, what's not convenient. Things like that."

As with other companies, Alberto-Culver made a significant effort to bring what it learned back from the field and share it broadly across the organization. It then translated those findings for employees so they would know how it affected their jobs. For this effort, Alberto-Culver leveraged the GDL network.

As we've discussed, the GDL program consisted largely of creating the GDL role, which acted as a conduit between the business and the leadership. GDLs also acted as mentors to the workers. Part of their mentorship role was to create "Individual

Economic Value Statements" (IEVs) with each of the team members they supported.

One informant described IEVs as "tying people's contributions . . . to business results. So if you think about it, everybody in this company leads to business results. The janitor keeps the floor clean, [which] stops from someone slipping, breaking a leg and they can't do their job. . . ."

IEVs really had an impact within Alberto-Culver. The company had the IEVs printed on employee badges so they were clear and accountable. When asked, executives and managers shared their IEVs with Gary (and those who weren't wearing their badges and therefore didn't have their IEVs with them were fairly embarrassed).

COMMON TRAITS OF EFFECTIVE MARKET OUTREACH

The four companies discussed thus far in this chapter did not use the exact same method for achieving this broad market outreach—Harley-Davidson and the almost universal customer connection experienced by its employees is an exception. But the different approaches employed by Marshfield DoorSystems, Harley-Davidson, Alberto-Culver, and Motorola had a number of common process steps that account, we believe, for their effectiveness (see Figure 7–2). They include:

1. Direct experiences with the market.
2. Broad acceptance of market messages by opinion/ functional leaders.
3. Company-sponsored ceremonies where these experiences are shared.
4. Translating these experiences into a Shared Market Understanding—or a "market schema." This Shared

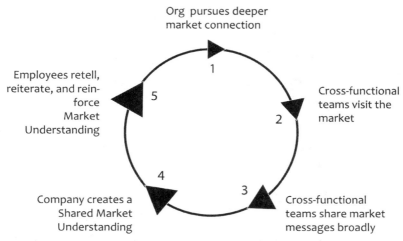

Figure 7-2:   Five Steps to Effective Market Outreach

Market Understanding is a common framework or definition of markets, segments, and value propositions that everyone understands and uses.

5. Retelling, reiteration, and reinforcement of market messages in day-to-day conversations.

From what we have seen, all five aspects are necessary to get the results needed to alter the mind-set that people had about the market and how the company served the customer. Together, they help create a holistic view of the customers. Taking just some of these process steps creates an incomplete view, and the result is akin to taking none.

Consider what happened at MediaCo as a case in point. Even before Bill Smith initiated the change process within the organization, MediaCo had hired McKinsey to run a project the company called "Market Focus." The purpose of Market Focus was to gain market insights and learn more about what the market—during the initial years of the Internet—would expect from advertising and media agencies.

An informant at MediaCo said the project was very secretive in how it was managed, and the resulting segments differed from how MediaCo had thought about its market up to that point. This difference was not a problem per se; rather it was the mode of communication and acceptance that really killed the effort. As one informant noted, "The segments they came up with weren't the segments that I would have picked—but they weren't bad segments. And had we taken that and started going to market in a different way two years earlier, we would have at least learned from the interactions with the marketplace."

In reality, the McKinsey segmentation work did not go anywhere or generate any in-house interest in further validating or connecting with the market. Looking back on the experience, the informant identified the external, consulting approach as fatal to change inside the organization. He said,

> We took people for like three or four months, held them way off line, and locked them up on this secret, confidential project. Went to the board and said we're gonna make all these changes and then we scrapped the work. . . . People were able to taint the results. . . . It tends to be the same big consulting formula, "We've got a lot of people who are really smart; who are off doing this study. You don't need to bother yourselves with it." . . . So McKinsey was off kinda doing stuff. . . . They come back and you get it and you're like, "Based on what?" And you can put any number of good resources against this project and you're still . . . not going to get aligned. . . .

The issue, in short, was not the quality of the information but the ownership of it. Fortunately, MediaCo recognized that the work McKinsey produced was relatively useless because the process steps around communication, translation, and repetition were not happening, and so internal employees were not embracing it.

As a result, when MediaCo had made some headway with change, they returned to engage the market with a slightly different approach that involved and integrated people from different departments in the company with outside personnel hired to help do market-oriented research and outreach.

One informant commented on this change: "These three teams are really fired up about owning this information. We have salespeople on it, we've got operations people on the team, we've got marketing people on the team. . . . They're not just being handed this deck and saying, 'Here's your structure—go do it.' They're conducting these interviews. They're going off with the consultants. They're doing the qualitative interviews. Totally eye-opening! Just mind-boggling to people what customers say. 'Oh! They want that? *That's* their problem?' To connect what we do with how our customers make money is a new way of thinking. You know? But once you know how what we do helps us make money, it gives us a whole lot of leverage that you never had before."

OPERATOR? WHEN OUTREACH PRODUCES FAILED CONNECTION

Not all the companies we spent time with had as much success with their efforts to reach out to the market, learn what the market wants, and translate that learning into a Shared Market Understanding that resonated throughout the firm. Some companies simply never made a real effort to reach out to learn what the market wants. Others tried to reconnect, but failed to gather meaningful insights or to share those insights broadly so that the firm could construct a Shared Market Understanding.

MediaCo managed a mid-course correction that allowed it to gain at least some understanding of its market. MediaCo never achieved the kind of organization-wide benefits seen at Harley and other companies, but there were some improvements.

BenefitsInc had a similar misstep at the beginning, but unlike MediaCo it was not able to recognize and correct the mistake. In brief, one of the groups at BenefitsInc attempted to reconnect to the market in similar ways to Marshfield DoorSystems and Harley-Davidson. The fieldwork initiated by BenefitsInc did not include a broad cross-section of functions, however. Findings were not communicated broadly through the organization, and there was no definition or crafting of specific customer segments, value propositions, or other concrete frames that allowed people throughout the organization to develop a Shared Market Understanding of who they served and what those customers wanted.

One informant from BenefitsInc remembered, "The first boss I had here believed that people should leave the office. He always thought the people at [divisional headquarters] really never left the office. So he wanted people to go out and do customer interviews. . . . He got all the people in [our location] who were in marketing within [the group] and they all went out and some salespeople too. . . . And they went and interviewed customers in Maryland and Virginia. . . . It worked out pretty well. . . . But the follow-up through some type of methodical 'What did we find?' didn't really ever get done—at least not that I know of. There were debriefings after we got back, but no formal report."

EquipmentCo had a similar effort, but as with BenefitsInc the field team consisted of a small group of functionally similar people for specific projects (e.g., product development) and experiences were not shared across the firm or embedded into organizational memory.

CONCLUSION

Businesses that progress far in the process of becoming more market-focused eventually need to develop a Shared Market Understanding, one that resonates and permeates throughout the organization.

We cannot overemphasize how important this step is to the overall success of resurgence. The process of reconnecting with the market allows resurgent firms to replace incorrect or conflicting definitions and ideas with consistent and accurate ones. By directly reconnecting, companies can create a common language and set of symbols to communicate within the firm. This process allows for more consistent selection and interpretation of important market information; greater accuracy in the transmission of that information across the firm; greater consensus in how to respond to the information; and an improved ability for multiple functions of the firm to respond in concert. More importantly, the reconnecting process creates intrinsic motivation in employees up and down the firm to serve the market; and it helps institutionalize cultural values through experience.

The companies that allowed cross-functional teams to go to the field and engage directly with customers and then bring those experiences and stories back to share broadly with the organization were most successful at creating that coherent and relevant Shared Market Understanding that is so crucial to what comes next. These experiences let employees see how their behaviors affect the customer and how their work contributes to the business and its ability to grow.

Only with that Shared Market Understanding can companies move on to the next step in the Reinvent stage of change: Collaborative Strategy.

8

COLLABORATIVE STRATEGY DEVELOPMENT AND IMPLEMENTATION

HARLEY-DAVIDSON HAD LONG BEEN AN ORGANIZA-
tion divided by functional perspectives but dominated by engineering. Prior to the leveraged buyout and the resulting turnaround
efforts, the engineering department had largely functioned as
an independent entity, answerable to no one. As one longtime
Harley-Davidson employee from the engineering division observed, "In the 1970s, the engineers developed the motorcycle the
engineers wanted."

In truth, prior to its change efforts the company did not have
a viable alternative to this departmental approach because it did

not have a single, accurate, and company-wide understanding of the customer. It is hard to collaborate if you have different views of your target.

When Harley-Davidson began using employees from all departments to staff the demo rides, however, people across the organization began having common experiences, which allowed them to develop a Shared Market Understanding. This experience woke the engineering department up to the possibility that other departments could contribute to the process of strategizing about the kinds of products the company should make.

The Harley engineer reported, "We started inviting the marketing people to our meetings, saying, 'Hey, tell us what needs to be done here.' And that was really the start, I think, of a very important part of the turnaround. . . . I think a lot of good things started to come together when we began to bring the marketing people into all the product planning that engineering was doing. . . . We realized that we needed the knowledge of marketing to do the right thing in the first place. To me, that's what's key. . . . First of all, you've got to have the right concept you're going to create, *then* you've got to do a good job of it."

MARKET-FOCUSED STRATEGY AS A COMPANY-WIDE EFFORT

Harley-Davidson's experience of seeing a formerly siloed process—such as product development or market strategy development—become more collaborative and integrated is typical of what happens in market-focused companies (see Figure 8-1). Significantly more people become involved in the planning effort, but the results are much better because everyone involved behaves according to a consistent set of cultural norms, and is operating with a Shared Market Understanding—of who the customer is,

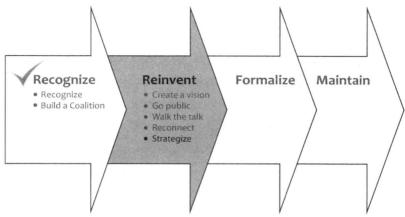

Figure 8-1:   Collaborative Strategy Enabled by a Shared Market Understanding

what he or she wants and dreams of, and even things he or she hasn't yet dreamed of. In effect, all the businesses we saw become more market-focused began adopting a simple formula that dramatically improved their prospects:

Market-Focused Culture + Shared Market Understanding +

Collaborative Strategy = Successful Programs

Today, this collaborative process of strategy and product development is the modus operandi of market-focused organizations like Harley-Davidson. In fact, one Harley-Davidson employee commented to Gary that the combination of a Shared Market Understanding, the collaborative nature of the organization, and a responsibility to fellow employees had evolved to such an extent that individuals were able to make organizational decisions with more confidence and empowerment than ever before.

"We have a pervasive, innate understanding of what customers/markets want," the employee said. "This creates an instinctive understanding about what the brand is about. . . . Some purchasing guy isn't going to go for [a] high-quality/low-price strategy and get plastic fenders for a Harley. He isn't even going to ask or discuss that option with anyone if a vendor offered. Why? Because he knows it is not Harley. Harleys don't have plastic fenders, so there is no need to waste his time on that . . . it's not going to happen. It's not part of the essence of Harley. . . . Pervasive innate understanding of the brand and our markets. It's kind of like being in church—you just know what to do when you're part of it."

Such a broad and diverse level of involvement in strategic issues is pretty rare in our experience. In most organizations, a small group does the strategic planning, product planning, market-focused strategy, and other important processes, with little input from others. The argument in favor of this approach usually hinges on its efficiency—a smaller group leads to stricter meeting management. Different groups are usually represented, but only at the leadership level.

But having more people involved is *not necessarily* less efficient. When the people in those meetings have different ideas about the market and who the company is serving, a lot of time is spent simply getting everyone on the same—potentially wrong—page. In contrast, when participants are all operating with a Shared Market Understanding, complete with a clear view of who the customer is and what his or her needs are, no time is wasted debating the definitions of different customer segments or customer needs. Instead, all participants are focused on identifying the best solution for that known customer, consistent with the value and promise of the firm. In the organizations we studied, once they developed a Shared Market Understanding, the number of people invited to participate in strategy and problem solving grows significantly and the solutions clearly improve.

Such collaboration would not be possible at an early stage of the process. Before the company has progressed in communicating and cultivating a new set of cultural norms and values and establishing a shared, organization-wide view of the customer and the market, it does not have the proper foundation to involve such a broad group in planning. But once those consistent, market-focused norms and views are in place, a complete transformation is possible.

The Harley engineer said that as a result of the shared experience of demo rides, people across the organization began to acknowledge the contribution that others could make. "It is very true and very pervasive in the company . . . that good ideas have their own life and their own merit—and it doesn't matter where they come from. If it's a good idea, it's valuable to the company. And also a sense that we're all in this together . . . just a sense that we are all part of the same thing here."

COLLABORATIVE PROBLEM SOLVING

At Marshfield DoorSystems, the cumulative effects of developing revised norms and values and developing a Shared Market Understanding had a huge effect on the employees' investment in teamwork. Now the company needed to focus its collaborative approach to develop a new customer value proposition that reflected the true need of the market and could guide all company employees in their work serving the customer, and the members of the value chain.

A group was assigned with taking what Marshfield learned from its customer-outreach effort and creating a value proposition that would close the gaps between what the customer wanted and what the business delivered. The value proposition effort highlighted four areas of focus for the company:

1. Late and incomplete orders
2. Excessive lead times

3. Inconsistent appearance
4. Specification deviations

The group also crafted a clear value proposition and posted it throughout the company as a driving motto:

> We supply doors and accessories to our customers that are: uniform and consistent in appearance, hassle-free, delivered on specified dates and times, for a premium price.

It would be difficult for us to overemphasize how important this value proposition statement was in the transformation of Marshfield. Marshfield DoorSystems management devoted enormous effort to ensure that everyone knew the value proposition and its relevance to their work. Hanging in all the public spaces at Marshfield DoorSystems headquarters were ten-by-twelve-inch framed copies of the value proposition, and informants pointed and referred to it during interviews. It served not just to align everyone but to remind them why they were there and for whom.

Once the value proposition team had completed this work, it needed to show progress toward closing the gaps between customer needs and what Marshfield delivered. The group decided to target length and width consistency as its first big project. Length and width variations created huge problems for Marshfield DoorSystems at the time. The industry has standard tolerances for length and width (namely, your door can be slightly longer or shorter than specified, but it is still compliant so long as those excesses or shorts are within a certain range). Despite meeting industry standards, Marshfield DoorSystems was not meeting the needs of the installers, and therefore it was not satisfying its customers.

A guiding coalition member recalled the progression of events: "We went back to the shop floor and had meetings with all the operators . . . including union representatives who visited the field. We said, 'This isn't management that wants you to do this, this is the customer who signs all of our paychecks.' So we created problem-solving teams. It was amazing what they found out. . . . That really got people pumped up to support the project and work together. . . . People on the shop floor know these things are going on, but no one's ever asked. You go beat up the saw operator for twenty years, 'The doors are sawed wrong.' Rather than doing that, say, 'Help us figure this out. This is what [customers] are seeing. Our data from when you guys measure doors in quality check don't show that. What's going on?'"

The cultural changes and a deeper, Shared Market Understanding set the stage for the Marshfield manufacturing staff to engage in a collaborative effort to find the problem with door sizes and fix it. "Their first inclination was that they checked the doors and it's all okay," said the guiding coalition member. "We got past that by sending some people out in the field to measure doors. They got all kinds of different sizes. So they were asking, 'How could this happen?'" Namely, how could the doors measure accurately in the shop and then be totally different in the field?

Seeing how the problem appeared to customers put the Marshfield DoorSystems manufacturing team in a new mind-set to find the problem. The informant said, "Then they went through the process, in reverse, trying to figure out what the problem was and found all kinds of things that affected the size after it left the sizing equipment. . . . Saw machines were doing a great job, but then there were a bunch of other things that were happening that affects the size of the door. So we had no problem sizing the door, but it kept changing size after it left the sizing equipment."

Meeting market needs through collaboration continued as Marshfield DoorSystems gained more experience with market-focused cultural values and applying the Shared Market

Understanding, with unanticipated positive consequences. Informants consistently said that the new organizational attitude and value proposition made market strategy development and implementation much easier. "There was one picture that we all focused on. And everyone knew it!" said one informant who worked on the shop floor. This same informant recalled what was, in her view, the greatest testament to the organization's change to market-based collaborative strategizing and organizing: "Basically, when Bill came, he turned the mill over to the people and said, 'This is your baby—make it work!' . . . [Today,] the union and the company are working together instead of against each other."

CROSS-FUNCTIONAL MARKET STRATEGY DEVELOPMENT

Along with the GDL program and the corresponding cultural supports, including the Individual Economic Value Statements, or IEVs, connecting people to the market, Alberto-Culver also pursued an active agenda to convert itself from a siloed and hierarchical company into a cross-functional, collaborative enterprise.

Part of the shift happened at Alberto-Culver as part of the leadership transition. Recall that Carol Bernick had just taken over as president from her father when the change effort began. In the months and years after her appointment, she spent a lot of time getting the right people as part of her leadership team. Many of her appointees shared her views about collaboration and team building, and it was their view that people at all different levels needed to be involved and engaged in making important plans. They needed a Shared Market Understanding before that engagement could be real, but once Alberto-Culver had invested the time to ensure that every employee had either firsthand or vicarious exposure to the customer, the company then progressed to engaging more people in marketing strategy and problem solving.

One Alberto-Culver marketing executive noted about the progression, "[It] wasn't difficult to get people going. If you establish a vision for people . . . and you say this is what we want to be when we grow up and everybody says, 'Yeah! That's what we want to be!' . . . then it becomes 'How are we going to get there?' And get *them* to figure out how we're going to get there. Then suddenly, it's *their plan,* not *my plan.*"

This same marketing executive emphasized how the company had changed since the Lavin era in the approach it took to developing *and testing* ideas for the market. He said, "Rather than dreaming up an idea and then going out and seeing how the consumers think about it . . . what we started to do is develop consumer insight among a wide variety of segments. Garnered from that, thoughts and ideas and concepts that would probably make sense, formulate them, *and then* go back and test them among consumers. [This] is a whole different approach, and I think that's really a key shift. Trying to get into the head of the consumer *up front.* Not by asking them, 'What do you need?' They'll never tell you what they need. By understanding what their habits and practices are."

This same informant later pointed out that the insights his department got from the field were not always easy to interpret. But after the transition there were a lot of people at Alberto-Culver involved in the process of connecting with the customer, deriving insights from that research and working to translate what they learned into effective strategy. An executive observed that the involvement of large groups in building strategy based on market insights made a huge difference: "There are no easy formulas to make this work. . . . But certainly if you're not doing it up front your odds of success are drastically reduced."

Collaborative Meetings at Alberto-Culver

Management investment in cross-functional cooperation was high all across Alberto-Culver—not just in the marketing function—and there were multiple cross-functional meetings established to allow people from different groups to collaborate on market, retail, and product strategies.

One typical example at Alberto-Culver was a daily logistics meeting chaired by customer service. The group convened every morning for an hour or less, with approximately fifteen representatives from customer service, logistics, manufacturing, and the warehouses. The meetings were open—anyone could attend. Occasionally, senior executives participated. A typical agenda might involve reviewing channel and service issues, making sure current and potential problems were handled. The group took ownership of each issue by offering ideas and solutions. Once the team reached a consensual decision, an individual or group volunteered to take responsibility for implementing the decision.

Gary witnessed a number of these meetings and saw firsthand the genuinely respectful and engaged interactions between participants. They were always focused on seeking the best solution for the channel. Outside the meetings, an informant shared that the members were empowered to take appropriate actions to solve channel problems or share ideas with individual channel members to save them money or help out in some other way. If warranted, they were empowered to conduct field visits or schedule meetings with channel personnel. That level of cross-functional interaction would have been unheard-of six years earlier.

The logistics meeting offers just one example of the kind of collaboration that evolved within Alberto-Culver. Both across functions and up and down the levels of the organization, people were encouraged to get involved and learn what was happening elsewhere in the business.

Another marketing executive said, "One of the things that was always extremely successful for me . . . [was] monthly business meetings with operations, finance, development, marketing, sales. . . . [It] includes everyone in the marketing group giving a presentation on the business: what happened for the month, what's happening this month. Then you've got development talking about new products, we have the agency coming in to talk about competitive advertising. . . . There are about thirty-five people that come; we run eight thirty to twelve thirty, and it's a way of connecting people with the business. . . ."

When Gary asked whether the participants were all managers, the informant responded, "Oh! *No, no, no!* It's the *doers!* Oh no, this is not a management meeting." He went on to describe one representative attendee: "She reports to a group director someplace, who reports to a VP, who reports to another VP, who reports to . . . my counterpart. . . . So she comes, she hears about the qualitative, she hears what's going on. And so she'll be part of the business. She'll hear about the customer thing that happened with Walmart or Kmart. It's just an example—that's how people are connected to the business."

Through such open meetings and efforts to bring insights from all over the company, Alberto-Culver worked collaboratively—horizontally and vertically—to determine the best way to serve the market and implement effective programs. The collaborative nature of this work and the speed with which the company could bring new programs to market were impressive compared to how the organization operated less than a decade earlier.

Teamwork and Collaboration at Motorola

Collaborative strategy development and problem solving were also at the core of how Motorola PCS pursued change. The organization invested hugely in the M-Gate new product development process and in the Executive Review Board (ERB), both of which mandated that personnel from all over the PCS organization be involved.

One executive informant said those requirements dramatically increased the number of people involved in strategy development and product planning, but the results were much better. "What you end up doing is creating a camaraderie that . . . may not have any effect at all on the definition of the product," he said. "But . . . you've got a team that can then work through normal process, which is more condensed. It's more focused. . . . What's fun is . . .you make sure that you're open-minded to those big sessions. That you could [reveal and learn new] stuff. . . . And that's a really wonderful surprise and great things can happen. . . . At one point . . . we had three hundred people involved in developing the strategy. And it was kind of like, 'What the hell are you doing?' . . . But it built a portfolio that was focused and clear and driven when we got done with it."

Informants credited the processes that Zafirovski enforced for embedding both the customer and collaboration into the way things were done—that "Market-Focused Culture + Shared Market Understanding + Collaborative Strategy" is the formula that all the successfully market-focused companies adopted to develop plans with greater potential for success. According to one Motorola PCS executive, the M-Gate process was "designed to really install some more discipline and formality . . . to become more market driven. So, as opposed to saying, 'I've got a product idea,' it starts with market intelligence and analysis. Based on what's going on in the external industry . . . what segments are you targeting in the market, and what's the opportunity to serve them? You start out with identifying the market segment and opportunity that you're going after and you use that to define a concept that goes before . . . the ERB, [which decides] what we put in the portfolio and what we don't."

Despite the enthusiasm we heard from informants, we were still skeptical about how collaborative Motorola planning was in practice. After all, for products to make it through M-Gate stages, they had to be approved by the five voting members of the ERB. With so few voters, it seemed possible that Motorola PCS was just replacing an engineering-centric culture with a sales-centric one. But that wasn't the case. The executive quoted above reminded Gary, when he asked, that it was cross-functional product teams that proposed and managed the products through the M-Gates to market. The ERB merely decided "go" or "no go" for each stage. Thus, the ideas and products that made it far enough through the M-Gate process to be discussed by the ERB were already supported by cross-functional teams pitching them for a given market segment.

He said, "The people, for example, in marketing and product line management and engineering and supply chain are working on these teams that get through [M-Gate]. So part of what we're saying is 'Your vote's implicit. You wouldn't propose a project to be put on the road map that you didn't believe in—we hope.' Seriously, right? I mean people get jazzed up and get passionate about it if they think it is a good idea. So we know they'd vote for their [proposed product]."

An employee from the design department at Motorola PCS shared with Gary how market-oriented values and a Shared

Market Understanding helped a product team gain consensus and work collaboratively. It wasn't an instant win—it took some work, learning, and trust until the design team got used to working with engineering, marketing, and other parts of the value chain. But, he said, "after three months, we really got on the same page and . . . most of all, having open minds to each other. Like me learning about the engineering constraints, marketing constraints, and program system constraints—and them taking on consumer perspective in how would we define the product positioning."

Increased collaboration allowed Motorola PCS to change the way it thought about the process of developing a product, from engineering to design to delivery. The various aspects were no longer viewed as needing to take place in an entirely sequential manner. Merchandising can sometimes inform engineering, not just the other way around.

For example, the design employee said, "I was in charge of coordinating all of the cross-functional workshops all the way to merchandising. It's like giving them a head start up front so they can do parallel process development instead of [waiting until the last minute]. . . . We had defined the product positioning . . . based on consumer values, not our values. Then, when people try to say, 'Oh, why doesn't that phone have a big display? Oh, why doesn't that phone have a bigger battery?' you can say, 'Because the target segment we're aiming for cares about the fashion aspect of the phone, or more about other coinage rather than the function of the phone.'"

The shift in process also improved the ability of Motorola PCS to think through how the various products in its portfolio would appeal to customers in different geographic segments. The Motorola PCS designer observed, "There's [also] a big value system difference between the regional markets. If you go to Asian countries or European countries, sometimes a handset means more than just making a call. . . . [In that way, it really helped] having more regional voices than in the past. We had more regional input about, 'You know what? That's going to work in Asia because consumers care about this and that and so on.' So, I think all those changes really made this [move] along. . . . Engineers sometimes would not know why we would have to make this one small or in this shape. . . . So it's really like the inner collaboration between . . . marketing and design and engineering . . . sharing one value. . . . [So instead of asking,] 'Why do we need to make this one small? Why do we need to think about this finish . . . because this is adding cost.' [But when] the engineers share the value, get it, they will be like, 'Oh, now we get it. We'll make it happen.'"

STRATEGIC EXPERIMENTATION

All the companies discussed thus far in the chapter approached development and marketing strategy by combining the Shared Market Understanding with collaborative strategizing. The result was far better, far more relevant product and marketing plans. Instead of operating by instinct or guessing what might work, they developed ideas, products, problem solving, and programs with a clear perspective on what the customer and the market needed.

Perhaps it should come as no surprise that after they developed a Shared Market Understanding, these companies were far more open to experimenting with new products and ideas, and far more willing to take on the inherent risk that such experimentation brings.

When Gary was doing the field research, one marketing executive he spoke to at Alberto-Culver was working on introducing a new product attribute to one of the company's product lines. This executive described the company's willingness to experiment with changes to products as fundamentally different from others he had seen, and directly related to the fact that the company had a Shared Market Understanding and a collaborative mind-set that encouraged involvement of different groups.

He said of the process, "[It's] not just a gunslinger winging it. . . . This is grounded in a lot of fundamentals. . . . We analyze all the competitors, we come up with a usage, we look at [contextual issues] . . . we can come up with rational explanation for a better [product attribute]. Everybody here can understand that. They can comprehend that and support that. Yet it's a risk—you have to change your product, yes, you're innovating—but the comprehension of the rational makes sense.

"That's not true in a lot of entrepreneurial organizations. . . . [In other companies I've worked with] you're continually having to explain why you think it's a benefit and why you want to pursue it. . . . In a company like this, people look at something like [this product attribute] as a big deal, something that could really be an advantage in the marketplace. People are excited about working on it. . . . 'Wow! You think we can get an advantage? What can it do for us?' Totally different mind-set. . . . And then, therefore, you end up being much more successful with innovations, ideas, and twists."

A marketing executive at Harley-Davidson communicated a very similar perspective about the importance of trying new things in the company and how the Shared Market Understanding ensured that those experiments were consistent with the values and the mission of Harley-Davidson. "The brand has to grow," the Harley-Davidson informant said, "and in order for the brand to grow you've got to do different things. If the brand isn't growing it's pretty much just dying. . . . The risk is finding new opportunities to grow. You're going to have risk. And that's why we're mitigating that risk.

"V-Rod is a perfect example. [V-Rod is the firm's first liquid-cooled commercial motorbike, positioned as a performance bike with a drag/road-racing heritage.] We wanted to find a new customer. It's part of growth. . . . Finding new customers may mean doing some things that are different—but you look at that bike, it fits the brand. I mean, we didn't develop something that didn't fit the brand. So [the product development team] had the responsibility of looking at that brand identity model and saying, 'Yep, this is right, this is right. . . .'"

Having a Shared Market Understanding does not ensure that new products or strategies are successful. It does, however, make sure that they are grounded in a deep, shared understanding of customer and market needs and wants, which mitigates the associated risks of such efforts. In the next section, we describe a company that did not seem to embrace that shared understanding when experimenting with a new marketing strategy—with disastrous results.

BUSINESS AS USUAL AT MEDIACO, BENEFITSINC, AND EQUIPMENTCO

Up to this stage in the change process, the companies MediaCo, BenefitsInc, and EquipmentCo had made efforts to engage in market-focused change and participate in each of the steps. Each company in its own way tried to create a change coalition, to revamp its firm's cultural norms and values, and to connect with the customer. Before these firms reached the customer-outreach stage, they had made enough progress that they maintained some momentum with their change efforts. But the failure of any of them to achieve effective outreach to the customer essentially halted change.

MediaCo, BenefitsInc, and EquipmentCo all made some efforts to reconnect with the customer, but those efforts were not cross-functional, they did not involve participants up, down, and across the organization, and the stories and lessons were not shared so that people who did not experience them firsthand could take part vicariously in customer outreach. As a result, some people within each organization gained some improved understanding and knowledge, but that understanding did not translate into a company-wide Shared Market Understanding. Without that shared understanding, as well as the goodwill and collaborative atmospheres that come with market-focused cultural change, there was nowhere else these companies could go. From our perspective, they essentially dropped out of the change process, cashing in on the limited benefits they had gained up to this point.

Their experience mirrors that of many companies that attempt to engineer a reinvention but fail to do it with a clear view of the market. One firm that is at the top of the business pages as we write this is JCPenney, the once-beloved department store.

As with Harley-Davidson and Marshfield DoorSystems, JCPenney's turnaround effort started when the company found itself at a financial crossroads. Department stores have been struggling for years to define their place in a retail market populated by discount stores like Walmart and Target on one end and popular specialty stores like J. Crew, Williams-Sonoma, and H&M on the other. A few challenges specific to JCPenney compounded these industry trends: the physical stores had outdated technology and design, resulting in cluttered product presentation; and the JCPenney's tradition of launching discount-based promotions—590 in 2010 alone—had undermined the integrity of the brand and pricing, such that the average discount increased from 38 percent in 2002 to 60 percent in 2011 while retail prices stayed flat. The company badly needed resurgence.

To its credit, the JCPenney board of directors recognized the need for change and hired Ron Johnson to be the new JCPenney

CEO. The fit seemed natural. An experienced retailer, Johnson had been part of the successful turnaround of Apple Computer. Apple is perhaps the quintessential resurgent firm, known for its near death in the late 1990s and its spectacular rise in the 2000s—in the fourth quarter of 2010 alone Apple Computer pocketed $4.3 billion in profits. Johnson was with the company through that resurgent era, and he pioneered the wildly prosperous concepts of Apple retail stores and the Genius Bar. Before coming to Apple, he had been part of a similar resurgence at Target, where he launched the well-known Design Initiative with brands like Michael Graves, Calphalon, Carr, and Bodum.

Johnson did what most CEOs do in the early months of a position when the excitement is fresh and they have lots of leeway to make things happen: he set out a vision. Johnson's goal was to "redefine the way America shops through a new experience and interface for retail." The corporate strategy he outlined focused on reinventing JCPenney as a specialty department store, complete with new store design and a new pricing and promotion model. The plan was ambitious and expensive, and Johnson put it into action after only three months on the job.

Up to this point, it could be argued that Johnson took some of the right actions, in the right order, to engineer resurgence. He was the new leader in a position to engineer change. He formed a team by bringing on seasoned marketing and operations executives whom he had worked with in the past.[1] Then he defined a vision for the "new" JCPenney.

What Johnson did not seem to do was examine the culture of the company he had inherited or investigate the needs of the market. What kind of company did Johnson take over? Whom did the people internally think they were serving? What was the state of communication and collaboration in the organization? Did customers even want a "new experience and interface for retail"?

There is no evidence that Johnson asked any of those questions, and there was definitely no effort on the part of the JCPenney organization to form a Shared Market Understanding from which a coherent strategy could emerge. It is more than likely that any such effort would have been viewed with disdain by the leadership team—Johnson famously inherited Steve Jobs's disregard for market research.

Despite that lack of insight, Johnson went ahead in February 2012 to launch the "Fair and Square" pricing and promotion model. Fair and Square was defined as everyday low prices, with one promotion per month. The company eliminated coupons, multiple markdowns, and other sales promotions.[2]

At the same time, Johnson launched the "Shops in Shops" design concept, which created a series of brand-specific specialty "shops" within each JCPenney store. The redesigned stores would be made up of around one hundred unique shops, each located on a "street" created from wider aisles. The space between shops would have computer stations, coffee bars, and other activities. Streets would terminate at "town squares," spaces with seasonal items and complementary services. iPhone checkout stations replaced cash registers. The idea was to turn JCPenney into a fun place to hang out—a "bazaar," in Johnson's words. The plan was to have all the stores redesigned by 2015, but JCPenney got started right away with renovations in key locations.[3]

Change was swift, but Johnson's strategy crippled the company's performance. During 2012, JCPenney shares dropped 17 percent and revenue fell by 25 percent to $13 billion, the lowest since 1987.[4] The company's S&P rating was downgraded to CCC+, with over $1 billion in store renovations still outstanding.[5] On April 1, 2013, Johnson was ousted just seventeen months into his reinvention effort, replaced by former JCPenney CEO Mike Ullman.

So what went wrong? On the surface, Johnson's strategy made sense. JCPenney probably needs to renovate the stores and update their look, feel, and presentation; it probably needs new pricing schemes; it can't be faulted for courting more exclusive, high-demand brands; and modernizing store technology is necessary and useful—focused technology change has been credited with bringing gains to retailers in the form of improved customer insights, better inventory management, and improved customer service. If Johnson was heading in that direction, what was the problem?

The problem lay with the market and the culture. Johnson set the strategy without first going through the process of creating a Shared Market Understanding, and then involving the wide spectrum of JCPenney departments with direct customer accountability. The ideas for what the new JCPenney should be were developed in a vacuum, devoid of valuable, diverse employee feedback grounded in that shared understanding. As a result, the Johnson strategy was weak and ill informed, and lacked any basis in why established JCPenney customers shop there.

There is also the challenge of culture. Customers do not just engage with design; they engage with people. The kind of wholesale store restructuring that JCPenney pursued would require a lot of support from customer-facing personnel—support that is possible only through the goodwill that accumulates when leaders make promises to employees in the form of demonstrated changes to culture and values. There are no shortcuts. Those changes need to be evident *before* turning the experience inside out.

To his credit, Johnson did make at least one cultural change early in his tenure: he eliminated commissions within stores so that store personnel were not competing against each other for a sale, or pushing product at the expense of what the customer said he or she wants. That was a smart move, but a premature one, as we will explain in Chapter 10.

Timing played a role in Johnson's failure in other ways. Johnson positioned his strategy as a long-term vision, but all the changes seemed to happen at once, from the "Fair and Square" pricing policy to store renovations. There was no time to work on the culture or test the ideas with customers. In just a few months Johnson launched wholesale changes to operations, pricing, design, strategy, and structure. It's no wonder the customer would feel alienated, to say nothing of employees.

New leaders are under a lot of pressure. Lauded for his success at Apple, Johnson likely felt that Big Change was his only option. He tried to model a JCPenney retail experience on Apple, a company that thrives in a cutting-edge, price-controlled atmosphere that has little in common with the low-margin, distribution-intensive, price-sensitive world of department store retail. Showing customers what they want worked for Apple. It doesn't work for a company whose product is available at another store down the street. Unfortunately, these strategic flaws came to light only after JCPenney lost $4.3 billion in sales.

CONCLUSION

Developing a Shared Market Understanding set the stage for different functions within Alberto-Culver, Harley-Davidson, Marshfield DoorSystems, and Motorola PCS to develop more deeply collaborative approaches to important business processes, from product development and marketing strategy development to strategic problem solving and experimentation. Developing a Shared Market Understanding was a precursor to this collaboration—without it, people from different business functions would not have sufficient common ground to strategize and develop ideas that were consistent with the values of the company and the needs of the market.

The most important outcome from this collaboration is that the results were better. Informants across all the market-focused companies consistently believed that they came up with better plans, introduced better products, and generally had a higher rate of success because of the combined power of having a Market-Focused Culture + Shared Market Understanding + Collaborative Strategy.

Sadly, not all the companies we spent time with were able to make this leap. The process toward market-focused change essentially stopped for the three pseudonymous companies because their efforts to reach the customer failed to create a Shared Market Understanding within those organizations. Without that shared view, collaborative strategy is impossible and the progress toward becoming more market-focused halts.

REINVENT

9

PINK SLIPS FOR DISSENTERS, OFFERS FOR BELIEVERS

BASED ON THEIR CUSTOMER VISITS, MARSHFIELD DOOR-Systems employees learned that customers needed the doors to be exactly how they ordered them and to arrive on time. After forming the value proposition team that developed a clear value proposition, Marshfield DoorSystems developed a new, market-focused philosophy for the factory. "First In, First Out" was very clear in its meaning—orders are fulfilled in the order they hit the factory floor. It may seem like a logical, even obvious, way to operate, but it was not standard practice at Marshfield, whose previous operating practice was to hew to a "hot list" that different people in sales put out, and which changed depending on the events of the day. First In, First Out was a major change for the company and required a lot of behind-the-scenes process adjustments to ensure that all the materials for manufacturing an order were in stock before that order was released to the plant.

Bill Blankenship and Jerry Mannigel understood the operational challenges. They also understood the psychological ones—the First In, First Out approach would require a shift in mind-set from different parts of the organization, and not everyone liked the shift.

The Marshfield vice president of sales, for example, was unhappy when the change coalition eliminated the hot list. Accustomed to getting his way, he simply ignored it and continued to move certain orders forward as he had done before. As one informant explained, "Most people jumped on board [the new train] right away. But we had to stop a couple of times and let people off."

In short, the sales VP—despite his senior position—was let go for his refusal to adopt the practices and norms of a changed Marshfield. The same informant said of the episode, "Our strategies were not consistent. [He] was giving value propositions and working in the total team lip service. But behind the scenes he was doing business the same-old, same-old—special favors for this and that . . . 'This customer is important, move him up,' etc. . . . The key to a value proposition is that you need both sides of the house to agree on the strategy and what they are going to do and how. They must be working with the same strategy. You can't have one side just giving it lip service."

Blankenship and Mannigel brought in a new sales manager who was committed to the value proposition of complete and on-time delivery for all orders. The first challenge was a backlog of orders, a legacy of years of hot lists and inconsistency in the factory. To clean out that backlog, everyone agreed to work on the oldest doors first, and the new sales VP gave a specific amount of time for each order to move through the plant.

Still, some workers resisted. "People said, 'Yeah, but . . . yeah, but . . . yeah, but,'" an informant said. "There were all these 'yeah buts.' Then Jerry Mannigel stood up in front of everybody and said, 'This is the way it is. . . . The first time you get caught *not* working on the oldest first, you get a warning. The second time you're fired.' Someone asked, 'You mean fired?' Jerry said, 'I MEAN FIRED.'"

Three weeks later, Mannigel fired the same worker who questioned the policy because he was caught working out of order. But Marshfield did not have to fire anyone else, according to the same informant. Within two months the factory had reached its goal of 100 percent on-time and complete.

THE COMPANY MUST CHANGE, THE PEOPLE CAN CHOOSE

At the beginning of the change process, few change leaders like to think about the possibility that they may have to fire people, least of all good people they have worked with for years. In fact, letting people go early in the change process can send a contradictory message to the workforce—you can't go public saying the company needs to change and everyone needs to be part of it, and then fire people. It erodes exactly the kind of trust and faith that allows leaders to make change happen.

It is also hard to know for sure early in the process who will make the transition and who will not. Every company has employees who fall very clearly in the "yes" or "no" camps for adherence to market-focused behaviors, just as every company has people on the margins, strong performers whose behaviors are not in line at the beginning with where the company wants to go, but who may adapt if given a chance. It is only in this last step of the Reinvent stage—after the company has reconnected with the market and reinvented the way it develops market strategy—that there is clear validation of what the market needs and what cultural behaviors are needed. Without that clarity, leaders can't know for sure which marginal employees to let go, let alone what qualities and values to look for in the new people hired to replace them.

There are, of course, exceptions that make layoffs necessary in the early days of the change effort. Layoffs were inevitable, for instance, for Harley-Davidson, which pursued change as a way to survive a catastrophic financial situation. (Immediately after the leveraged buyout, the thirteen owners instituted layoffs that reduced the Harley workforce by about 40 percent.)

But Harley was an exception. None of the other companies we studied made such drastic reductions in the workforce in the Recognize stage of change. Those that successfully engineered their own resurgence did not specifically work to change or reinforce the culture by culling the workforce until late in the Reinvent stage, after all reasonable effort had been made to allow existing employees to adopt new behaviors. By this point in the change process it was clear which employees were sincerely invested in change, and which were simply playing nice but behaving in ways that were contrary to the values of the organization (see Figure 9-1).

Cutting the Cancer—Removing Dissenters for the Health of the Company

The decision to let someone go is a difficult one, and many companies whose survival is less urgently threatened than Harley-Davidson's was may have trouble taking actions against employees who do not conform to the new rules. This is especially true for companies that are beginning to see evidence of resurgence in the

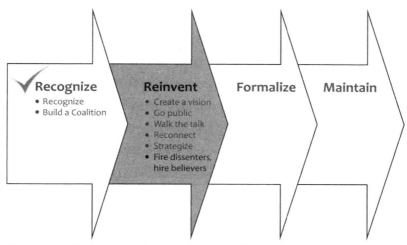

Figure 9-1:   Enforcing Culture by Firing and Hiring

form of new behaviors and cultural norms, more collaboration, and more effective, customer-focused strategy.

Yet issuing pink slips is necessary. It is even inevitable. There are always going to be some people whose ideas and values complemented the pre-change organization, but who are completely antithetical to your emergent, vulnerable, market-focused culture.

One executive at Alberto-Culver described the experience: "We had to understand that not everybody *can* and not everybody *will* play. In our [group], we turned out forty percent of the people. But we did it with great humanity because *those watching* were interested in what we were doing to their peers. . . . But at the same time it hurts like hell . . . when I have to turn one loose. I know if you don't do that—I think it's the biggest mistake we make as managers—if you don't cut out the cancer, it will hit your organization broadly."

A Marshfield DoorSystems executive described the same issue in slightly different terms: "It's not a choice for the organization— we have to change. It's only a choice for the individuals."

The above quotations illustrate a point that many senior leaders made—namely, that letting people go is hard to do, is completely necessary, and should be done humanely.

Employees were given the opportunity to adapt to the new culture, reflecting the value placed on people. The firms all made sure their team members heard the message about the company's change efforts; they were given opportunities to attend any training or development programs put in place to help people embody change; they made sure all employees had every opportunity to adapt. The companies that progressed to this stage also made clear that continuing with the old mode of doing things had a non-negotiable consequence—dismissal. Ambiguity at this stage of the game is disrespectful. Be clear about the consequences and don't give too many chances. There comes a time in every change effort when it is clear who supports change and who does not. Leaders need to be unanimous in their support of removing employees who do not buy into the firm's new vision and are not exhibiting the new norms and values.

Leadership buy-in is critical. As one Alberto-Culver executive said, "You'd rather have management support, but you at least had to have management permission. That was demonstrated, it was tangible, people could see that I had permission from the organization to make the changes."

Issuing pink slips to employees who do not behave in ways consistent with the new norms and values is easier with employees who produce average or below-average output. It is less easy and obvious for high performers or longtime contributors, especially salespeople or other customer-facing professionals who consistently achieve their numbers. It is not an easy decision, but keeping employees whose behavior openly challenges the firm's change effort sends a mixed message that undermines change, regardless of that person's status in the company. If an employee's behavior is out of sync with the new values, he or she must be replaced with a better fit.

STOPPING THE TRAIN TO LET PEOPLE OFF

Many firms lay off *some* people and/or make personnel shifts throughout the change process. Building a change coalition by its very nature tends to elevate some people over others. The catalysts of change can also force companies to let employees go, as in the case of financial hardship that requires mass layoffs. There will also be people who choose to leave on their own.

Even very senior people may choose not to be a part of where the company is going. As we have already mentioned, two members of Harley-Davidson's original change coalition left and were replaced early in the change process. A third LBO member decided to *remove himself* a few years after the buyout occurred. According to reports from people who were there at the time, this situation was, strange as it sounds, an act of real commitment to the future of Harley-Davidson. The situation came about due to a disagreement between this coalition member and Vaughn Beals about the direction of the market. When it became clear to the coalition member that he and Beals would not be able to agree, he offered his resignation for the sake of the group; he even declined other positions within the firm. This is less a case in which a person removed himself because of cultural dissent and more one in which an employee *believed in the culture* and the organization with such commitment that he chose to leave rather than threaten the collaborative environment that was evolving.

All the companies that engineered a successful resurgence gave employees an opportunity to remove themselves early in the change process. The big public events and subsequent culture training at Alberto-Culver, Harley-Davidson, and Marshfield

DoorSystems were designed to send a clear message about where the companies were going and what leaders expected of those who remained.

The decision to stay is not always easy or devoid of sacrifice. The financial issues at Harley-Davidson required the company to reduce wages for the staff members who remained. Vaughn Beals promised that when the company turned around he would give the money back, but there were no guarantees. One informant said, "Nobody really had any confidence of that at the time. But when things came around, he did give the money back. And that was really a major point, if you were there and went through that; Vaughn made good on his word and you got your money back." Not everyone stuck around long enough to get their money back. Some chose to try their luck elsewhere, and those who stayed were making a real commitment to stay with the firm for the long haul. As one informant described it, "The people who were here during that time *were here because they wanted to be*. No question about it."

Public events and unpopular actions, like pay cuts, can be viewed as passive messages—they allow employees to draw implicit conclusions for themselves. But it would be wrong to assume that companies need only initiate these indirect approaches to effectively cull the organization of cultural dissenters. On the contrary, the same informant who made the comment about people wanting to be at Harley-Davidson also said that it was known within the salaried ranks that failure to adhere to the values of the company and, particularly, to follow through on commitments, would result in dismissal. It is not clear how many, if any, employees Vaughn actually fired individually, but the perception remained in the organization that cultural norm violations were unacceptable.

Likewise, an executive at Alberto-Culver explained the explicit process that he and other leaders went through to select who would be invited to stay and who would be asked to leave. This executive described the situation: "We looked at people and we said, 'Look. There's a change that's going to occur. A significant change. The bar's going to go up high, hard, and fast. We looked at and evaluated you in depth. We *don't* think this is consistent with who you are.' We didn't go up and say, 'You're a lousy employee.' We said, 'Here's how it'll happen. You stand at a crossroad. One way says, 'I'm gonna jump on this thing.' The ladder's against the wall and we will probably overcompensate to make sure you get up that ladder. But you need to know that if you miss a rung and fall off the ladder, you are off the ladder.' The other side of the crossroad says, 'Here's a soft landing. . . . *You have your choice.* They *are* mutually exclusive.' And people opted, for the most part, to take the soft landing. We did a lot of work to validate our case as to who could and who couldn't play."

As is clear from the examples of Alberto-Culver and Harley-Davidson, these companies actively communicated with their employees about what was happening and what the expectations were for those who stayed. At Alberto-Culver, most people who were told that their past behavior did not conform with the new organization made the decision to leave. But there will always be some employees in any company—like the VP of sales at Marshfield DoorSystems—who remain and openly refuse to change. It is at this point—after efforts have been made to create and implement a change vision and reconnect with the market—that they need to be let go.

BIG CHANGES IN PERSONNEL

In some companies, the turnover in personnel—even senior personnel—was dramatic. Seventy percent of Carol Bernick's direct reports were replaced in the first few years of Alberto-Culver's change effort. Some of these leaders were part of her initial guiding coalition and then were elevated to new positions as part of senior leadership. Others were recruited from outside the organization because they had functional competencies and were a strong cultural fit. As one guiding coalition informant recalled, "[Carol] really feels strongly, and I absolutely agree with her, that she needs people who really understand the culture and who operate within the culture. . . . Obviously you've got to perform in your function, but you have to understand and support and drive the culture into the organization."

To replace those who did not fit with the new Alberto-Culver, Bernick recruited people who already had a way of working that was in line with the cultural changes being made. Gary had conversations with many of the newer executives in the Alberto-Culver organization, and when he asked them about the collaborative team meetings that Alberto-Culver had instituted as part of its change effort, they often tilted their heads in confusion and said they had always worked that way. Hence, apart from removing people who did not fit the new culture, much of Alberto-Culver's success at becoming more market-focused was attributed to bringing in people who already believed in the culture and were able to add to it through their unique experiences and competencies.

We mentioned the resurgence that took place at eBay as a result of that company reinventing itself to more broadly fulfill its mission as a matchmaker between ecommerce buyers and sellers. John Donahoe, the CEO who led that effort, took a similar approach to Bernick's in building the team he needed to make change happen—there were some shifts and additions when he first took over as CEO, but those continued as the nature of change needed became clear. Four years into his tenure he had replaced most of eBay's senior management team. He has said, "A significant change in senior leadership was necessary to take eBay to the next level."[1]

Motorola PCS saw some similarly dramatic changes in personnel. Informants at Motorola all noted that the majority of people reporting to Mike Zafirovski at the time when Gary was there doing fieldwork had been in their positions for less than one year. An informant commented, "Mike Z's staff, if you look at it, there's like two people who have been here more than ten years. I mean, he just cleaned house in like three months."

It may sound brutal and dramatic, but "cleaning house" for some organizations is the only way to address legacy behaviors that work against the new market focus. At Motorola, the infighting and conflict were so integrated into the way work was done that Zafirovski had no choice but to let people go who did not conform to the new collaborative processes.

An executive from Motorola spoke about why such dramatic personnel changes were necessary: "I preach this a lot here, we spend more time fighting amongst ourselves than fighting the competition. So changing that type of mentality is something that I continue to strive to do to the organization and that the organization continues to move forward on. But it's hard, because when people have been ingrained to think a certain way, changing that . . . trying to get organizations to change their current culture, their current way of thinking, it isn't something that happens overnight. Sometimes it only happens painfully through a market downturn, or painfully through firing people that refuse to change, or through reorganizing yourself to try to do things differently. But that's what we have to do and trying to get people to realize that that's what we need to do is a challenge that all of the leaders in our organization have to step up to."

The Motorola people who stayed exhibited support for the market-focused change embedded in the collaborative processes implemented in the organization. Specifically, Motorola informants noted that the defining qualities of the employees who stayed included not only a high level of competency in their area of expertise but also an ability to adhere to the cultural values—such as working the matrix and keeping commitments.

PERMITTING DISSENTERS—
WHEN COMPANIES DON'T ISSUE PINK SLIPS

We've discussed the importance of removing dissenters who refuse to adhere to the cultural norms of the changed organization. We've also quoted multiple executives from resurgent companies talking about how difficult and necessary this process is to the momentum of change within the firm. Despite this clarity, some organizations find it too difficult to do.

A number of executives from MediaCo, for instance, talked about how resistant that organization was to removing dissenters—even those people who were openly known to operate in ways antithetical to a market-focused culture. One executive said, "Even when we do workforce reductions or try to scale back, people end up in other areas. It's not my analogy, but this is one I use, it's the water balloon analogy. You squeeze to get people out of here and they just pop up elsewhere. So we worry as an organization. We're like, 'We don't have a job that fits Mark well.' Or, 'Mark doesn't get it, he needs to go, *but* Mark's been working all these projects, Mark's done all this work.' We're worried that Mark will end up at Competitor X."

The MediaCo executive specifically referred to concerns about the risks to institutional intelligence as a reason why employees with long tenure or other forms of personal equity are not let go, even when leaders know they aren't a good fit. But he was quick to add that protecting competitive intelligence was not the only argument for keeping someone.

"There's always a reason," he said. "[Someone will say Mark's a] 'friend, good guy, worked hard,' et cetera. *'But he hasn't delivered the results.* . . . But maybe we haven't given him a fair chance.'

"So it's hard for us here to let people go. I had people who worked for me and managers and I was trying to get managers to get someone better in here. It was really hard. They just couldn't understand. . . . [They] feel bad, but that's a bad investment. I would tell managers, 'You need to invest in people who can have a long-term impact.' And they feel bad. People here care a lot about other people. They don't realize that by not making those changes, it's not good for the employee either. Because someone at some point is going to come in and make that change. You're better off doing it now than letting them spend ten years here at mediocrity, but that's the culture."

Although he did not talk about it explicitly, this MediaCo executive also highlighted the frustration that people who are supporting the culture feel when employees are allowed to stay while resisting change. He did not have the permission of leadership to make the changes he needed, and Bob Smith in the wake of leadership upheaval did not appear to have the degree of consolidated power he needed to make decisions about removing executives. As a result, MediaCo made very few personnel changes, which contributed to the failure of its change efforts.

HIRING FOR CULTURAL FIT

Removing dissenters from the organization addresses one remaining challenge to cultural change, but it also exacerbates another— namely, how to screen new hires to make sure that they fit the values and culture of the company.

The people who decide to stay and change with the firm have a particular level of commitment and understanding of what market focus is and what it is not—because they have lived through the change process and they get what the new culture is all about. But the same cannot be said of new people coming in. Since in many cases they will not have seen firsthand what the company was and what it became, the expected behaviors and cultural norms may not be as resonant. Leaders responsible for new hires will have to do some screening and look for certain qualities in the people who come in. It is not enough that they be high performers; they need to perform at a high standard in a way that is consistent with what the business stands for.

One Motorola informant from the design department spoke about how he screens potential hires and said, "I hire people based on the fact that they're here to do three jobs. One of them is to do world-class design. One of them is to develop those processes and systems that are required to do world-class design. And the third one is to be a cultural change agent."

Elaborating on that point, the informant clarified his view of design as uniquely equipped to effect change in a positive way. He said, "Because we work collaboratively between marketing and engineering, and have a viewpoint on strategy, we are useful in terms of cultural change. We're useful as people who . . . hear a literal engineer pounding for something that doesn't make sense from this perspective and to gently find out whether, in fact, design is misunderstanding what it's about. Or whether there is something about the positioning of it [that isn't understood or agreed upon]. It takes a mind-set."

That position, in his view, requires a particular approach to working with other groups that is more exploratory than combative, and he looks for that exploratory mind-set in the people he brings into his team. "When people say no, your first reaction has to be 'Why do you say that? How is that?' rather than 'You suck, you ignorant dick, you don't get any of this stuff.' Cultural change is all about you never hear no. All you hear is a need for a different tactic, a different approach to solving problems."

The Motorola designer is speaking about his specific needs for a very specific company, but the broader message is that market-focused resurgence requires companies to screen potential employees not just for skills but for cultural fit. They will need to have values and a way of working that are consistent with those the firm has been working to establish and promote.

Screening recruits for cultural fit doesn't just benefit the business, though businesses do benefit enormously—recruitment, hiring, and onboarding cost US companies an estimated $124 million per year, lost funds if a recruit doesn't work out.[2] Cultural screening is also consistent with the market-focused value of respecting people. It is not fair to bring someone in if they aren't going to make it in the organizational culture of the business.

One informant from Harley-Davidson noted that the company culture had become so strong that "you are either assimilated or rejected. If you respect the organizational culture [you're okay], versus if you want to change everything, then the organism rejects you."

Another informant from Harley's technology department noted that the organization screened its recruits for cultural fit along with skills. "You need to be able to work with people. Before, our interviewing was about what do you program in and just ask them if they were successful. [Now,] all these other things about communication, getting along with others, et cetera, are all very important. They are also about how you get things done—not just if."

CONCLUSION

Working to change the behaviors of the employees you have seems to effect change earlier in the transformation process. But there comes a point when it is clear who has embraced change and who has not. At this stage—usually after the company has engaged in focused outreach to reconnect with the market—the emphasis on coaching cultural dissenters ends and companies that engage in successful resurgence abandon the effort to change behavior and shift instead toward removing dissenters.

At this stage resurgent companies also invest in screening potential hires for cultural fit as well as competency. Screening makes it more likely that new members will positively contribute to the culture, that they will be comfortable, successful, and productive, and that they will stay with the firm for an extended period of time.

Removing dissenters and hiring believers allowed for an incremental jump in employees acting in ways that are consistent with the change pursued by the firm.

10

MAKE IT OFFICIAL

Formalize, Reward, and Indoctrinate

ALBERTO-CULVER WAS GOING GANGBUSTERS. THE GDL program had dramatically improved communication and morale in the company. The channel specialists were finding new and creative ways to increase channel sales. The company had been pursuing its change efforts for a few years, and the results were increasingly evident. Everyone seemed to be operating from the same understanding of the market. Things were going great! Which is why the new vice president of sales, hired specifically for his reputation as a market-oriented manager, was so surprised when a few of his sales representatives confronted him and his management team in the days before the annual sales meeting. The tension was thick.

The problem lay with the incentive package. Alberto-Culver offered a variable component to most people in the organization as a way to keep everyone aligned with and focused on meeting the needs of the market. Like most companies, Alberto-Culver tied the variable component for sales personnel to each individual's performance relative to his or her own targets. This is standard practice in most industries, and yet it was at the root of the problem. The entire organization was supposed to collaborate to meet the market, but the salespeople were all rewarded based on individual performance.

"You're killing us by trying to put together the incentive program on an individual basis and get it all right and make sure everybody's indexing on the right growth for that customer," the sales reps told the VP. "We want one number. All of us. One number."

The head of sales consulted with all the salespeople individually to see if this view was pervasive. He concluded that the Alberto-Culver sales force broadly agreed that if sales were a team effort, people should be compensated according to that philosophy. The VP decided if they wanted one number, they would get one number. But what should the number be? Market growth at the time was at 2 percent, so management formulated the sales team's variable compensation to include a 3 percent minimum threshold, 5 percent target bonus, 8 percent maximum, and a 13 percent threshold for a group trip to the Caribbean—including significant others.

A sales informant told Gary of the result, "Now, what do you usually do in a sales incentive program? You get a couple tenths of a percent over to ensure you got it and you stop, right?" Instead, Alberto-Culver in the first year realized 18 percent annual sales growth against the bonus ceiling of 13 percent, and saw 11 percent growth against a bonus ceiling of 10 percent the following year. Delivering such remarkable growth required the collaboration of everyone across the firm, but the passion of the salespeople and their efforts to change the compensation structure to support the firm's evolving culture suggest an amazingly strong investment in formalizing a market-centric culture.

FORMALIZING CHANGE THROUGH FORMAL STRUCTURE AND REWARDS

Employees who are part of a market-driven change effort are often motivated in the early stages of change by the intrinsic need for survival. Those who work for companies experiencing financial stress are all too aware that their jobs depend on a successful resurgence. They weren't worried about bonuses—they were worried about being employed. Those who buy into the potential for resurgence are often energized by the relevance of what they are doing. They are a part of something, contributing to the survival of the company.

Such intrinsic motivation can carry a team of change agents pretty far. There comes a point in every turnaround, however, when a business needs to alter its organizational or operational structures to be more in line with the facts on the ground of how it does business.

For many, it may seem counterintuitive to change the organizational structure or compensation mechanisms *now*, once change is already well under way. Common business wisdom suggests that compensation, restructuring, and rewards mechanisms should be part of the motivational tool kit in the early stages.[1]

Yet our research shows that companies don't really need compensation changes at the beginning; the people who genuinely buy into the change effort have the intrinsic motivation to take the right actions. The extrinsic component is stark: job or no job.

People who don't buy into it aren't going to behave right no matter what you throw at them. Only later—when proof of change is beginning to show in the form of higher sales, higher price per sale, greater market share, faster customer acquisition, lower unit costs, or whatever your preferred form of measure is, and when employees see such concrete proof of change—does the organization enter the third stage of the change process, when they need to *Formalize* change (see Figure 10–1).

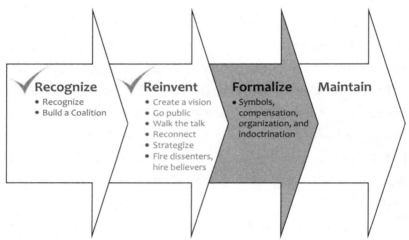

Figure 10-1:   Formalizing Change through Symbols, Compensation, Organization, and Indoctrination Practices

At this stage, companies need to take steps to hard-bake changes into the organization by documenting and defining values and norms, implementing appropriate compensation schemes, altering organizational structures, and ensuring that onboarding or indoctrination programs are in place to help new employees adopt the right cultural behaviors.

SYMBOLS OF MARKET ORIENTATION

We have pointed out the ways in which the companies we profile invested in changes to culture and behavior as a foundation for their change efforts. We noted as well the way these cultural values were emphasized—through public communication, modeling by senior executives, and other implicit and explicit means. As important as these demonstrations are, the cultural norms and values had not been formally documented and publicized prior to this stage of change. Up to this point, companies that successfully achieve a turnaround have reinforced their new cultural norms through behavior. But there comes a time when resurgent organizations need formal artifacts or symbols of change, and many of the companies we have seen do that by formally defining and publishing their values.

Alberto-Culver explicitly defined its cultural values two years after instituting the GDL cultural change program. As an informant noted, "[We] had a real concern with losing what made us what we were. . . . We came up with the idea that we should have corporate values. We should not only have them, we should infuse them throughout the organization. . . . We built them into our performance process. We continue to use them every way we can so we don't lose sight of them. They're just not something you create one time, a mission statement, and stick it on a door."

Making the values explicit ensured they were formalized into the firm. Once explicit, there was an ongoing process to ensure they remained salient to all members. As Carol Bernick commented, "I mentioned that we want people to memorize our list of ten values. It's in our [annual employee] survey ('Do you know our corporate values by heart?'). Do I trust people to answer that one honestly? I do; if people can't answer it when they get to the question, they've since looked it up. This is an open-book test."[2]

Harley-Davidson formalized its cultural values when Richard Teerlink became CEO of the company in 1988—more than six years into its change efforts. At that time, Teerlink said he "perceived the need to tie together the organization . . . on the level of values, philosophies, and vision."[3]

As part of the effort, Teerlink launched a set of brainstorming sessions, which helped identify the shared values of: tell the truth, be fair, keep your promises, respect the individual, and encourage intellectual curiosity.[4] These values reflected the firm's implicitly understood core values, but were formalized to preserve them and explain them to new members.

By formalizing the core values, organizations make them explicit to all employees and ease the transition of new employees who did not experience the change firsthand.

COMPENSATION STRUCTURES FOR MARKET-ORIENTED FIRMS

In addition to formalizing norms and values, change must also be formalized through the firms' compensation and rewards systems. There is no single compensation mechanism that works to reinforce or encourage a market orientation. The "one number" model that Alberto-Culver adopted to formalize its change efforts with its sales force would not necessarily work somewhere else. The story we used at the beginning of this chapter is not prescriptive, but illustrative of the way that changes in compensation are often necessary in order to reflect changes in culture and values.

Harley-Davidson significantly altered its review and compensation systems in the early 1990s to reflect the organizational changes it had undergone. Note that this happened almost *ten years* after the leveraged buyout catalyzed the change efforts. The firm was enjoying increased revenues, profits, and market share, but these gains came with new tensions as employees felt the disconnect between the new market-oriented culture and the formal incentive structures, which had remained more or less unchanged since the early 1980s.

In *More Than a Motorcycle: The Leadership Journey at Harley-Davidson*, Richard Teerlink, the president who succeeded Vaughn Beals, and Lee Ozley wrote, "Employees argued that, at the end of the day, the 'real' work of Harley-Davidson was the work that the company recognized in a paycheck. This 'touchy-feely' stuff seemed okay . . . but the organization would resist the kinds of behaviors that were being proposed until the company recognized and rewarded those behaviors."[5]

A management review of existing policies, cultural goals, and employee perceptions uncovered four conclusions that served as a guide for a redesigned compensation and evaluation program. Paraphrased, those conclusions were: people are inherently motivated and want opportunities to act on that motivation; salary and benefits are important, but not the only way to reward and recognize good work; people want to be fairly compensated, both in relation to their peers within the firm and in relation to similar positions in other companies; and rewards and recognition should be consistent with company values.

Based on these guidelines, Harley-Davidson changed the employee evaluation and compensation structures. To start, it implemented a new personnel development system called the Performance Effectiveness Process, or PEP. PEP aimed to link individual objectives with the work group, business unit, and corporation; provide employees feedback to understand how their behaviors squared with the company's expectations; and provide a development opportunity for employees to improve their performance. PEP was directly tied to the Harley-Davidson business process, which directly tied the corporation's values, vision, and objectives to business unit missions and operating philosophies, which were then connected to unit objectives, annual strategies, work unit plans, and, finally, PEP goals.

PEP was strikingly similar to Alberto-Culver's GDL and Individual Economic Value processes in the way it embedded an employee's individual roles and responsibilities to the larger organization and the market.

Employees were given a great deal of autonomy to determine what was best for the organization within the broader umbrella of its values and objectives, without having to make trade-offs between individual compensation and the welfare of the organization.

Along with the PEP evaluation system, Harley-Davidson management also adjusted compensation to include a higher variable component. Prior to this change, only the top seventy-five managers had a variable component to their compensation packages. A holdover from the AMF era, the variable package focused only on financial measures, with no eye to strategic activities or operational excellence. Harley-Davidson changed all that, believing that any successful change needed to be fair and reflective of the new environment at the firm. Harley-Davidson expanded the variable program to include all salaried employees in 1990, and all employees by 1993. Bonuses were paid to *everyone* or *no one*, based on the goals of the company, which were defined at the business unit or plant level. Management also altered the program so that financial measures represented 30 to 70 percent of the variable; strategic or operational measures made up the remainder (e.g., quality levels). As the final piece of the program, management instituted quarterly, and then monthly, meetings with employees so that they could have a clear picture of how they fared meeting their objectives.

The key part of the change in compensation for both Alberto-Culver and Harley-Davidson was an emphasis on fairness and on rewarding employees for adhering to cultural values, while still preserving intrinsic incentives and individual motivation to collaborate.

WAITING TOO LONG FOR COMPENSATION CHANGES

If there is any doubt about the necessity of adjusting compensation systems at this stage of the change process, the experience of Marshfield DoorSystems should be enlightening. Marshfield also saw huge improvements from the change efforts it pursued in the mid-1990s. But by 2001, the company was still using the same compensation scheme as it had before its transformation, and people were getting frustrated.

The tension was evident at one set of meetings that took place in early 2002. The meetings began with a formal presentation by executives and managers, during which the presenters communicated business results and talked about ongoing strategies and tactics. There had been a precipitous drop-off in orders following the terrorist attacks of September 11, 2001, but Marshfield Door-Systems nonetheless realized record sales and profits by selling higher-value doors and services in the declining market.

This was an amazing accomplishment. But the third shift union employees in the 4:30 A.M. session did not clap or show any enthusiasm when they heard about it. Later, at the 6:45 A.M. first shift meeting, salaried workers clapped in response, but hundreds of union employees did not.

During the question-and-answer session for the first shift group, an employee stood up and asked, "What are you going to do about the attitude problem in the mill? We keep hearing about money, money, money, but what's in it for the union?" This question was met with enough clapping (and some catcalls) to suggest a large portion of union members felt similarly.

A senior executive responded, "My understanding is that the biggest concern has always been that people want paychecks every week. Our goal is that people are all still employed here in one year."

In fact, the question was not a total surprise. The previous day, one executive informant had said, "It's one of our scripted questions, 'The company had a record year. How come the Christmas bonus was cake and ice cream and a coffee cup?' Generally, there is a feeling that the owners and VPs are getting all the rewards from the sweat of the hourly workforce."

Employees were frustrated that, in spite of the cultural assumption that everyone should work together to meet and exceed market expectations, there were two distinct groups when it came time to distribute the results of those efforts.

Management was not ignorant of or ignoring the situation. At the time, they were developing an organization-wide variable compensation scheme that had not yet been unveiled to the vast majority of employees. Multiple informants said they had envisioned such a scheme from the beginning of the transformation, but wanted to wait until employees were comfortable with their ability to work within the new culture and had experienced success. There was particular concern that union workers might see variable compensation as a scheme to take money. But the deployment of the new scheme was delayed by a number of organizational changes.

The fact that tensions got so hot at Marshfield DoorSystems illustrates the frustration that can arise when employees feel a lack of alignment between the values and their compensation. Alberto-Culver and Harley-Davidson likewise experienced those tensions and reacted—fortunately before the issue grew too acute.

MARKET-ORIENTED ORGANIZATIONS

Adjustments to organizational structure may also be necessary to formalize change at this stage. Again, timing your reorganization at this stage—often years after change efforts have begun—may feel counterintuitive. So many companies reorganize in the early stages of change because they believe a new organizational structure is part of the explicit and implicit incentives that employees need to act in culturally appropriate ways. Yet we do not believe those early changes help. On the contrary, they probably hurt the effort.

Though it may be uncomfortable, it makes a lot of intrinsic sense to hold off on reorganizing until a number of changes are already under way. At the simplest level, it is really hard to know what to reorganize into if you have not yet reconnected with your customer and your market and established an accurate Shared Market Understanding.

The companies that successfully became more market-focused and reaped the results did not usually create huge and explicit organizational changes in the early stages of the change effort. Any reorganization that happened took place at this later stage, once cultural shifts had already taken place and the organization already had a strong and coherent view of the market.

For example, Alberto-Culver's Carol Bernick had done some shifting when she first took over, but that seemed less part of the change effort and more her effort to consolidate her leadership power. Once the issues of morale and market challenges became clear to her, the major change was not one that showed up on the org chart. Her Workplace 2000 group instituted the GDL program and inserted GDLs into the existing structure of the organization to create this parallel channel to improve communication and reset the cultural norms.

Later, Alberto-Culver took more substantive steps to shift the organization in ways consistent with its market-oriented outlook. For example, it created an autonomous customer service department (customer service had previously been part of finance) and explicitly linked customer service to marketing and logistics so that all relevant players in fulfilling customer needs were embedded with each other.

Motorola PCS also saw some organizational shifts in the early months and years of its resurgence. But there again, those changes more accurately reflected the matrix organization that Mike Zafirovski liked to lead. While this approach *later* helped reinforce the communication and collaboration that the organization needed, no one at Motorola credited the matrix for the cultural changes it experienced. As we said in the previous chapter on vision, it was really the use of the M-Gate and Six Sigma processes that forced people to engage and communicate.

Harley-Davidson instituted the most dramatic organizational changes of the companies we spent time with. Survival was top of mind for the first five to eight years of Harley's resurgence. But once the company had stabilized and was seeing improvements, management decided in the early 1990s to assess whether the organizational structure was allowing it to get all it could from its people. Richard Teerlink, Harley-Davidson's CEO from 1989 to 1997, has written, "Harley's people had learned that customer needs can change dramatically and quickly. Just getting good at solving last year's problems was no longer acceptable. . . . What Harley needed was to get the right people together, at the right time, to do the right work right. . . ."[6]

Harley-Davidson decided to reorganize the company according to what Teerlink referred to as "natural work groups"— essentially clusters of people who take on different parts of the critical internal processes that allow the business to bring value to the customer. Since those processes change depending on the needs of the customer, the work groups need to be coherent when they are together yet flexible enough that they can morph and shift.

The result was a "circle organization," a flat, cross-functional structure comprising work groups led by functional leaders. In its

1998 annual report, Harley-Davidson described its circle structure by saying, "The senior management group is divided into three broad functional areas called circles—the Create Demand Circle, the Produce Products Circle, and the Provide Support Circle. The management science behind this approach is an organizational design that promotes interdependent work teams."[7]

Harley was sincere when it called its circles interdependent. Each circle was linked to the others through a Leadership and Strategy Council (LSC). The LSC was made up of representatives from each circle. Those representatives were voted in by the members of their respective circle, and LSC representation rotated every two years so that different leaders had an opportunity to represent their group in the work of the LSC, which was to collaboratively develop policies, make high-level resource decisions, and advise the CEO.

One executive said that with the circle structure, "It's the opposite of living in a silo. Everybody knows everything—whether you like it or not. Everyone has a right to ask, 'What are you doing on this?' And we have enough venues for that to happen."

Another Harley-Davidson director commented on the necessity of collaboration within each circle. He said, "When Rich [Teerlink] put us all in the circles, there was no rule book. They just said, 'Here you go. And here's the philosophy around it.' So I think there was a lot of struggling . . . a lot of trust and communication has to happen."

The circle organization that Harley-Davidson adopted did not cause its resurgence. It merely solidified the market-oriented collaboration and teamwork that allowed the survival and growth of the iconic motorcycle manufacturer.

Regarding his attitude about circles, Richard Teerlink wrote, "The Harley organization should be only as complicated as it absolutely needed to be . . . [and] should derive 'organically' from the functions the organization needed to carry out. We didn't want to draw boxes and lines on org charts until it was clear exactly what the organization needed to do. And . . . when the time came, the employees themselves should decide on the specifics of those boxes and lines."[8]

INDOCTRINATION

Shared experiences allow the employees who participated in the early stages of change to adopt the right behavioral norms. These people are part of the change; they feel like they own it, and the firsthand experience of knowing what things were like before and how they've changed into the "now" can provide a really powerful foundation.

Like all experiences, however, the saliency of those firsthand experiences can degrade over time. In addition, as firms continue to recruit believers, there are more new employees who did not enjoy the firsthand experience of going on customer field visits, participating in value proposition meetings, or attending workshops aimed at teaching people how to collaborate and engage in culturally consistent ways. The culture may set the behavioral norms, but not all employees and managers have the optimal level of knowledge or skills to employ consistent behaviors.

To address these challenges, firms often create formalized training programs in order to indoctrinate new employees and to reinforce the culture through skill development for existing employees.

Alberto-Culver's GDL program remained at the core of its change efforts, even in the Formalize stage. GDLs reminded employees about the core values of the firm, kept employees engaged, and ensured their personal development. Every employee had a GDL, so all new employees were indoctrinated through the same system. GDLs provided mentoring and guidance, ensuring every employee was taken care of and nurtured within the organization. Alberto-Culver monitored how well the GDL program achieved its goals by using an annual employee survey, alluded to by Carol Bernick earlier in this chapter. The annual survey included questions about whether each employee knew the company values, had an IEV connecting them to the market, and felt their GDL was offering the necessary support and cultural guidance.

Alberto-Culver had the good fortune of hitting on a system that served its purposes both in the early days of change and as the change process progressed through to formalization. In contrast, other companies that successfully became more market-oriented needed a new set of rules for the later stages of change.

At Marshfield DoorSystems, for example, there was no formal "onboarding" or new-employee orientation program. Because of the company's relatively small size and low turnover, however, new employees could be acculturated on a more personal level. They could meet with employees from different departments, share meals, etc. For example, during a senior staff meeting in August 2001, executives had a conversation about the departing summer interns. The interns were discussed by name, and the executives could share their views on which ones they wanted to hire after graduation.

Marshfield DoorSystems also adopted a number of institutional training programs in order to reinforce the cultural norms of collaboration and problem solving. To that end, during 2001 the company formalized training programs in *kaizen* and Lean manufacturing concepts. The training goals were to advance employee empowerment by providing conceptual tools to redesign their work.

One executive explained, "We want to get to the point where everyone asks, 'What do the customers want?' And then they take action to make that happen. Before, the plant/division was very top-heavy with innovations and directions. Now we're releasing demons, lots of little demons—and they're good demons. And they are asking questions and considering the customer everywhere and making improvements. The key is that we don't have to talk about it! [The result] is naturally occurring improvements all the time."

There was a parallel training program for senior and middle managers aimed at cultivating greater knowledge, understanding, and skill levels to "be fast and in control" as the organization responded to and drove the market. Gary sat in on and observed the first forum focused on managing organizational change and strategy development. The forum provided participants with new tools and a common language with which to discuss them across the organization.

The combination of kaizen and Lean training programs for plant employees and leadership forums for managers appeared to further formalize the shared values of a market-oriented culture within Marshfield DoorSystems. Lean training programs reinforced collaborative teamwork in the plant and provided new conceptual tools to proactively redesign organizational processes to better serve market needs. Leadership forums similarly reinforced collaborative teamwork among managers, while providing additional conceptual tools for managing employee concerns around change.

CONCLUSION

As companies move to formalize the changes they have made to their culture and values, they may need to align compensation mechanisms and organizational structures to better reflect the collaborative, team-oriented, and market-focused activities of the company. All the companies we have seen successfully achieve a resurgence eventually made some shifts in these areas, but the key is timing—none of them made changes to the organization or compensation early in the change process, before they knew what the market wanted and what behaviors they would need to reward.

Companies that make it to this stage are ready to begin the process of passing the responsibility for cultural regulation down to the people most able to affect the experience of the customer—the employees.

STAGE III

FORMALIZE

11

POWER TO THE MASSES

DAYTONA BIKE WEEK HAS BEEN A MAJOR EVENT FOR Harley-Davidson enthusiasts since its inaugural run in 1937. Harley-Davidson owners love to show up in Daytona and show off their customized Harleys. Even during the worst years, a Harley presence in Daytona was a point of pride.

Gary had the opportunity to participate in Bike Week in 2002 as a volunteer "employee" for Harley. While working the rides, a customer approached Gary and asked if he could park his customized V-Rod in the demo ride waiting area so people could admire it. Harley-Davidson riders show a lot of pride in customized bikes, both their own and others'—it's an important part of the culture. The V-Rod was a new product at the time and there weren't a lot of customized models around Daytona at the time, so Gary thought it would be a great opportunity to showcase the new model and see riders' reactions. But since he wasn't a *real* employee, he didn't feel like it was right to make the decision. So he asked the customer to wait a second so he could find the demo ride manager.

When Gary found the manager and explained the situation, the manager was clearly confused—why don't you decide, he insinuated. Gary said he was uncomfortable making that decision. The manager explained his thoughts about whether parking the bike in the Harley-Davidson parking area was okay. He suggested a few questions Gary could ask, but Gary, again, insisted that it wasn't appropriate for him to make the decision. Finally, the manager came out to meet the customer, spoke to him, decided it was okay, and then tracked Gary down to tell him why he made the decision he did. As Gary listened he realized that the manager was making sure he understood what was going on so that next time he could—and would—handle the decision himself.

POWER SHIFTS

Gary's experience at Daytona Bike Week demonstrates the way that market-focused change enables a shift in expectations about who has the authority to make decisions that affect the customer. It would have been unheard-of before this process for a manager at Harley-Davidson, Marshfield DoorSystems, Motorola, or Alberto-Culver to expect a junior-level employee to field a request from a customer and make a decision about it himself. Part of the deep dysfunction of so many struggling companies is that the employees with the most direct contact with the customer have the least power to positively affect his or her experience. All the decision-making power resides with the most senior executives.

Changing this top-down power structure takes time. At the beginning of the change process, the employees are not ready yet to be accountable to the customer and the executives don't want to pass it along to them. Executives are not holding on to power just for the sake of it, but rather because the culture is not yet at the stage where the leadership can trust people to make decisions that gel with the values of the firm and its goals for addressing the market.

Only after the guiding coalition has created a vision, changed norms and values, established a Shared Market Understanding, and reinforced expected behaviors through compensation mechanisms and other formal means is the foundation in place for employees to take on greater authority. Having used their power to drive the organization through the first two stages of change, guiding coalitions appeared to turn over that power to individuals within the culture (see Figure 11-1).

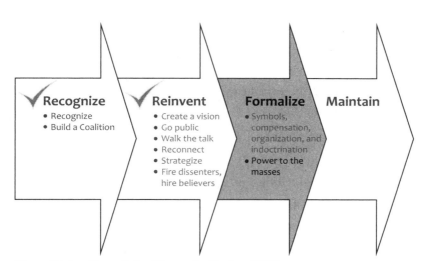

Figure 11-1: Formalizing Change by Passing Off Power

Culture Serves as the Platform for Change

The relationship between technology platforms and associated applications offers a useful metaphor for the way that executives hand over the power for delivering direct customer value in market-focused companies. High-tech companies like Microsoft build platforms such as Windows, and independent software vendors like Adobe build specialized software products to perform certain functions. Microsoft's productivity applications, such as Microsoft Word, Excel, and PowerPoint, have been very successful in their own right, but not even Microsoft has the capacity to create all the best-in-class applications for the PC. The lesson from its expensive also-rans (think Microsoft Money) only reinforced that it benefits far more by creating "developer tool kits" that allowed independent software vendors to build applications—both for servers and PCs, and now also for mobile devices—that ran on Windows. The software vendor could concentrate on making its product the best it could be, and Microsoft could benefit by selling more OS licenses to that vendor's customers. Apple has brought that same model to an entirely different level by publishing tools that allow developers to create Apps that run on the iPhone and the iPad.

What does this have to do with formalizing change? Think of all the efforts up to this point as the platform, the Windows of change—the leader, the change coalition, the values and behaviors they encouraged in order to change the culture, and the core reconnection with the market that defined the Shared Market Understanding. The people working in direct contact with the customer, in contrast, are the Apps, the effective tools that give direct benefit to the user. Nonexecutive employees at all levels, especially on the front lines, provide the immediate functional value for the customer, but their programs won't work at all if they are not aligned with the foundations of the platform. Change one line of code and you get a malfunction.

Early in the change process the bugs are all over the place, but by the time when companies are formalizing change, all those kinks are out. The employees know the culture inside and out; they live it. They understand implicitly what is expected of them. They are, to use the metaphor, experienced developers of platform-specific Apps.

Power, Not "Empowerment"

An executive at Harley-Davidson explained what happened at the firm by saying, "Everyone owns the brand. So what we do is make sure that everyone understands what the brand is. And if they understand what the brand is, they should be able to make decisions on the brand. They're *empowered* to make decisions on the brand. Now, empowerment is knowing when you don't have the skills to be empowered."

Most companies and managers who speak of employee empowerment mean that employees are responsible for outcomes. That was true at Harley-Davidson as well, but the difference in firms that are not market-focused is that employees are not given any latitude to make decisions based on independent interpretations of the situation or their own strengths and weaknesses.

In contrast, the kind of power seen at Harley and elsewhere comes after the employee has been equipped with strong cultural cues for how to interact with colleagues, customers, and channels, and has context on the details of strategy for the firm. Together, these platform elements give the employees the tools to make effective decisions.

What the Harley executive quoted above is saying, and what Gary experienced personally at Daytona, is that employees are not only allowed to make autonomous decisions—they are expected to do so. More importantly, they are prepared for the task. The work done to create a shared culture of collaboration and to establish an accurate, Shared Market Understanding prepares employees to make decisions that are consistent with the values and norms of the business.

Gary heard from other employees at Harley-Davidson about their experiences seeing the company change from a top-down structure, in which all decision-making power resided with the LBO team, to a culture in which employees in all functions were expected to make decisions for themselves about the best way to serve the customer. This effort to empower the customer extended to union workers, an amazing change considering the formerly contentious relationship between the company and its union.

This change was perhaps most inspiring for the way it made people love their work. One manager who had been with the company since the 1990s said this about the way decisions were made in the "new" Harley-Davidson: "We're not talking about anybody going off on their own here. But we're talking about understanding the business process and having ideas that would creatively leverage it and having the freedom to champion ideas, get other people involved in them, such that it would be [a] teamwork process."

Another executive said, "One of the things I see about Harley is, we're all ordinary but we come here and somehow get motivated to do extraordinary things. That's what Harley is about: ordinary people doing extraordinary things. And some very good and extraordinary people [are] in there too, as there are everywhere. But even ordinary people do great things here. Why is that? Once you've gotten people to do great things, you can't put the lid back on. It doesn't work. Once people are empowered and know that they're somebody, and have *made things happen* by being somebody, they don't want to go back. Nobody does. I don't either."

At the core of the extraordinary Harley was the group dynamic in play within the organization. Another informant said,

"The participative environment, I think, was remarkable because of the amount of effort [management] put into trying to include all the employees—not just the salaried people—but all the employees.... It's a system down there right now [at the Kansas City plant] where the union leadership works right with the company leadership. They call it the leadership cube. It's half management people and half union people. The governance system there gives the union workers control over decisions about how they think they can do their job the best. Not complete control, but gives them a lot of influence on that. And it's something that's being tuned going forward, I mean, to start something like that that's not commonly done, that there's no real good example to follow, you learn some things as you go along."

It was also implied, as part of the shift of power toward employees, that any effort to improve the experience of the customer could include communication that moved back up the chain of command. For example, Gary heard that a service department employee had learned of some issues from customers in Daytona that he believed needed the attention of then-CEO Jeff Bleustein. So he called Bleustein and left him a voice-mail message, which Bleustein then shared with other members of the management team. The level of individual employee empowerment at Harley-Davidson had reached the point that it was okay—even encouraged—for anyone to call the CEO with a concern. That level of access is unheard-of in almost any other multibillion-dollar enterprise.

TOOLS TO FACILITATE POWER SHIFTS

The other companies that reached the stage where they could Formalize change encouraged a similar shift in power and autonomy from senior management to the more junior employees directly responsible for bringing value to the customer.

We mentioned in the previous chapter that Marshfield Door-Systems was training employees in kaizen and Lean manufacturing techniques as part of its effort to formalize its market-focused perspective. One benefit of this investment was that it equipped plant workers with the skills they needed to solve problems and address customer needs autonomously. One informant described a situation in which a facilitator worked with a group in the shipping department.

"We had seen a large number of claims, complaints, and frustrations about products not being packaged properly," the informant said. "Our biggest problem was distributors complaining that 'it wasn't packaged how I ordered it.' So we had this blitz going on . . . hourly people along with the supervisor."

As part of the kaizen effort, a few representatives from the shipping department sat down with one of the salespeople. Annoyed, the salesperson asked why they were having such a problem providing a service that the distributors had paid for. A light went off. According to the informant, one of the hourly people said, "Wait, let me see. Am I to understand this right? We know they're paying for palletizing, but you mean some kinds of packaging cost more than others?"

The salesperson answered, "We have twenty different ways of palletizing, and there's twenty different prices. Whatever you ask for has different prices."

The people in palletizing didn't know that. They just thought that some clients wanted it one way and some wanted it another. "A lot of times we're busy," the informant said, explaining the logic of the palletizing team. "So we figure, what the hell is the difference? I'm doing the next pallet; I'll do it just the same. We think one is just as good as the other. We think the plywood in the box is just a waste of money anyhow."

By engaging with the salesperson, the palletizing team real-ized how they create value for the customer. They also saw how they were caught in the middle between the salespeople, who were trying to offer more options to the customer, and the shipping de-partment, which for the sake of efficiency and simplicity wanted those options reduced to one.

"They didn't realize the two were causing problems for each other. The salespeople didn't understand some of the associated costs. Even though they were charging differently, it wasn't appro-priate relative to what the costs really were. So the solutions came out and the rest of that week they spent their time understanding every single one of the options. This is the pure cost of it. So we have a markup or discount and everybody knows it. Now they know why, so when they get a request for palletizing in a certain manner, [they understand] this is what the customer wants."

This experience shows the increasing level of collaboration and autonomy held by employees within the organization. A strong culture and a shared understanding of the market were critical to enabling this collaboration. In addition, the guiding coalition had to be behind this shift, encouraging individual employees to act independently and collaboratively to make decisions.

Autonomous decision making extended much further than we had expected—even to the employees making personnel deci-sions. Business dipped dramatically in the wake of the September 11 terrorist attacks, and Marshfield DoorSystems had far more capacity in its plants than it needed. The approach of the "old" Marshfield would have been to announce layoffs to deal with the shortfall and to allow the union to let the most junior people go, regardless of skill level, reliability, or other factors. Everyone agreed that this method left a lot to be desired, so the manu-facturing department decided to try something new. Instead of instituting mandatory layoffs, it implemented the model of *discretionary* layoffs whereby the department first identified the plant areas where it had overcapacity and then asked if anyone wanted to volunteer for two weeks off. The company continued to pay for health care and contribute to their 401(k) during the discretionary period, and it gave manufacturing more flexibility to flex personnel up or down; this flexibility came in handy because orders were on the rise again within months. According to one Marshfield DoorSystems executive, the company would not have had the people it needed for the rising demand if it had had to lay people off—it wouldn't have been able to hire them back when the company got more work.

This creative solution was noncoercive, homegrown in the manufacturing department, and consistent with the interest of the company in respecting its people and creating a collaborative environment for creating value.

EMPLOYEES ENFORCING CULTURE

As power and authority shift to the employees, so too does the responsibility for maintaining and enforcing cultural norms and values. In the early stages of change, the guiding coalition members act as the primary models for the kind of behavior and values they feel the organizations need. Organizations that did not have those consistent leaders-as-models didn't make it very far along the path toward a market focus. During the Formalize stage, however, the leaders pass the responsibility for maintaining the market-focused culture down to the employees.

The meritocratic nature of Alberto-Culver's GDL program created a seamless transition between the leaders modeling market-focused values and the GDLs carrying the responsibility for maintaining it. Carol Bernick observed, "Having real power to make change is part of the reason people don't consider it a bother to be a GDL. Quite the contrary: it's an honor. And it's not something that comes automatically with a certain rank; we have GDLs from every rung of the management ladder. The people who serve as GDLs have been handpicked for qualities like empathy, communication skills, positive attitude, and even the ability to let one's hair down and have fun."

One of the reasons why the GDL program works so well is because the GDLs are very accountable to the people they serve. We described in Chapter 6 how Alberto-Culver used rewards and recognition as a way to positively reward those who were Walking the Talk of change. GDLs who were actively working to foster collaboration and respect in their group invariably ended up carting armloads of rewards back to their offices after an annual meeting. That kind of visual accountability helped not only in the early days of change but also later, when the company was working to formalize the norms and behaviors it needed to maintain the cooperative and collaborative atmosphere it had built.

This means that in a very real way GDLs are not the only people with power to influence the business and the culture—everyone has power. If discussion and other methods of resolving differences fail, or if violations of the culture cannot be resolved, employees can utilize their collective power by taking responsible GDLs to task through the employee survey. At many companies, employee surveys are pro forma documents that everyone fills out but that mean nothing. Not so at Alberto-Culver. As one informant noted, "There is retribution available for a disgruntled employee that isn't available in most companies."

Marshfield DoorSystems employees were also empowered to enforce cultural adherence at all levels—even to the top. At one point during the Formalize stage of Marshfield's turnaround, management had been failing to communicate as actively as they had done during the Reinvent stage. One union member called them out on it. "We used to get communication all the time," he said. "We used to have meetings every morning . . . until two years ago. . . . I think there is an issue of communication here. . . . What are the monthly profit numbers? Shipping on time—we used to get this weekly. What has been shipped on time and complete every week? . . . We used to also get orders in every week."

Surprised by the communication degradation, an executive replied, "If you're not getting updates, we need to do an audit of what's happening." He assigned the task to another executive and the meeting moved on.

These experiences and others show that as firms become more market-focused, employees become empowered to enforce the culture.

Motorola: Still on the Path

Up to this point in the chapter we have not said anything about Motorola and what it did to pass power to the people providing direct value to the customer.

The truth is that we don't know. Motorola had not yet progressed to the point of formalizing its change efforts at the time of the fieldwork. One Motorola executive acknowledged that the company still had a way to go, saying, in somewhat cryptic language, that the company was getting a lot of insight into its business and the needs of the market through its efforts to reconnect with the customer, but that it would take "two to three cycles" of that kind of insight (which he clarified as taking two to three years) before it would translate into and influence deep cultural change.

The situation at Motorola was nonetheless enormously improved in the time we spent with the company. Motorola PCS had made real and sincere progress in breaking down functional barriers and encouraging collaboration. Yet it is no secret that Motorola PCS again stumbled in the late 2000s and was eventually purchased by Google. It is possible that the failure to capture value in the smartphone is rooted in a failure to formalize change by passing the power to the people. Given how long the combative culture had reigned and how ingrained those behaviors were, it is possible that the company never felt that the market-focused cultural platform was secure enough to allow employees to act as independent developers within it.

CONCLUSION

Part of formalizing change involves distributing authority to make important decisions. Power is no longer consolidated with the leadership and the change coalition, but is distributed to the people most able to add direct value to the customer. At this stage in the change process, the cultural norms and behaviors should be so firmly ingrained that employees at all levels of the company know how to behave and what guideposts to use to make decisions that are consistent with the company's goals and values.

From here, resurgent companies progress into the fourth, and last, stage of change: Maintain.

MAINTAIN

12

STICKING WITH CHANGE

Employee, Market, and
Cultural Maintenance

WITH THE MARKET-FOCUSED RESURGENCE WELL UNDER way—even, by some interpretations, complete—it is almost inevitable that people forget why the company needed to change in the first place. As employees leave and new ones join the firm, a declining percentage of employees experienced the change firsthand. Even those who had firsthand experience with the transformations sometimes develop conflicting interpretations of how or why the shift took place. The most common tendency is to mythologize one person as the hero of change. At Harley-Davidson, that change-god was Vaughn Beals.

One informant who experienced the transformation said, "Vaughn was very much command and control. And when the boat is sinking or the plane's on fire, I don't want to hold a committee meeting to figure out what we should do. I want someone to tell me, 'Hey, you, grab that bucket and start bailing water out of the boat,' or whatever. . . . Vaughn got us through the bailing-out-the-boat period."

There is no doubt that Vaughn Beals was a commanding presence at Harley-Davidson—informants never varied in their view of him as a forceful and decisive leader. But the "Vaughn got us through" view discounts the role of the other twelve owners, to say nothing of the hundreds of Harley-Davidson staff members and union workers who participated in and embraced the cultural changes necessary to turn Harley-Davidson into a market-oriented organization that sought out and listened to customer feedback. Beals's successor, Richard Teerlink, and other executives who worked with or followed Beals at Harley-Davidson believed that in order to maintain the changed culture they had cultivated, they would need to take corrective action against such mythologizing that elevated one lone figure above the collective actions of the group.

MAINTAINING CHANGE

Anthropologists have long documented the tendency of human beings to develop myths—and elevate mythical figures—to accommodate or explain our understanding of life's events. *The Iliad,* recognized as the first work of modern Western literature, was one such effort to document and reconcile a major destructive event and claim its heroes, and villains, as they choose—Achilles, Odysseus, and Agamemnon; Hector, Paris, and Priam.

This tendency to mythologize is neither a good nor a bad thing. If anything, it is a basic human way to formalize lessons and apply them in new situations, which can be positive. The challenge for companies like Harley-Davidson, where mythologizing focused on elevating a central figure, is that it can threaten to remove the power and agency from the employees who are, in fact, in charge of taking customer-focused actions every day.

It is understandably tempting to attribute change to one figure, especially in organizations that have an authoritative and charismatic leader like Vaughn Beals or Carol Bernick. Some organizations have two such figures—also at Harley, the designer and Harley-Davidson scion Willie G. Davidson was long held up as a kind of cult figure. One longtime Harley employee offered a case in point of the way people talk about Willie G.:

> He creates something, like Frank Lloyd Wright created or Buckminster Fuller, which gives you a way of living. It really does. The difference is that Willie is not the kind of person who lacks modesty like Frank Lloyd Wright and Buckminster Fuller did, who took their massive genius into areas that, sometimes, were a bit odd and eccentric. But Willie G. Davidson has always stayed steady and *has always designed motorcycles that people want* [emphasis added]. Folk artists are what riders are and he understands that, so he gives them something and then really watches as they change it and doesn't intervene. I'm talking about some pretty sophisticated stuff here. And it is him. He is the driving force. . . . You've got a very quiet, unique, very artistic individual who really is the tribal leader inside and out. So that part of it is real. Willie G. Davidson is that important, that essential, that real inside employee culture and outside, in rider culture. He's the bridge that fills the gap between the two cultures.

As this quotation illustrates, mythologizing can be dangerous to change because it gives credit to one person and lessens the contribution of others. In reality, it was the work of the group and its collaborative commitment that made the transition into a market-focused company possible. Mythologizing threatens to shift accountability away from the people who do the work toward the leaders. By the logic of the myth, if Willie G. or Vaughn Beals is the force that makes Harley-Davidson customers loyal at that tribal level, then no one else needs to contribute—market focus will happen with or without the actions of the many.

Of course, Beals and Willie G. did not create change alone; similarly, BenefitsInc, EquipmentCo, and MediaCo—all of which had clear leaders spearheading change but little consensus in the ranks—could not effect change by influencing only small factions of the organization. Such centralization of power and contribution simply doesn't work in a market-focused organization. Power flows from the leadership to the employees. It's a one-way road, and if employees do not use that power effectively, a firm's momentum suffers, and lack of momentum can easily slip into stagnancy.

Companies that maintain a market focus work hard to prevent mythmaking and other revisionary views to seep in and invade the

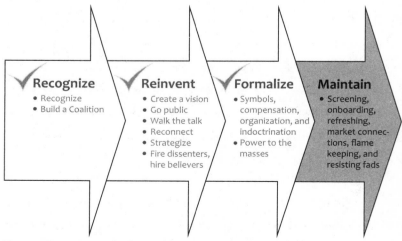

Figure 12-1:   Maintaining Change

culture of the company. Though companies with hugely successful turnarounds like Harley are vulnerable to their effects, those same firms can take conscious steps, which we'll review in this chapter, to dilute those threats as they arise (see Figure 12-1).

REVISING HISTORY—WIDESPREAD MYTHMAKING

People are not the only objects of mythmaking in a post-turnaround world. The company itself, certain functional departments, and even relatively minor strategic decisions or investments can sometimes be viewed in retrospective terms that differ dramatically from the reality. As we saw in Chapters 3 and 4, the *pre-transformation* Alberto-Culver, Harley-Davidson, Marshfield DoorSystems, and Motorola, as well as the other subjects of the original study, were defined, even crippled, by a lack of collaboration, a lack of communication, and confusion and opacity surrounding the key strengths and focus of the business, among other issues. Yet years later, when the companies are through the turnaround, there are not enough people left in the firm who remember those realities. A new, rose-colored version replaces the original reality.

For example, Harley-Davidson informants who had joined the organization in the 1990s, after the market-focused change had been formalized, had dramatically different views of the pre-turnaround organization. One informant asserted that Harley-Davidson had always been close to its customers, saying, "From everything I've read and everything I've understood— miraculously over the last hundred years there's been this very similar philosophy. AMF kind of disrupted that philosophy, but then the people that were actually here tried to continue to process that philosophy in spite of AMF. . . . So I think it's just an evolution of it. I think it's just a matter of focusing on who we are. Who is Harley-Davidson and what can we do to make experiences better? What can we do to keep our current customers happy and bring more people to it? By nature, our philosophy has always been we listen to the customer. Why not listen to them? We talk to them all the time. We ride with them—we're there, interacting with them. We're not going to ignore them. . . . But I don't think that changed in 1984. . . ."

The assertion that Harley-Davidson has always been close to its customers contradicted not only the view of people who lived through the AMF years and beyond, but also the history of the company. Demo rides did not exist until 1983–1984; there was no broad employee contact with customers before then. The customer contact that continues to this day is a direct result of the demo rides and the establishment of the Harley Owners Group, or HOG, which has its own set of rides and events throughout the year, managed from the beginning with the same volunteer approach as demo rides.

Despite this documented history, informants who joined the company in the 1990s insisted that Harley-Davidson's core success depended on the *long* tradition of external rider culture: "There's the institution of Harley-Davidson, which is rider culture. That will go on—it has been going on—no matter what the business does. . . . What happened during AMF was the institution refused to be colonized by the business and then developed its own homemade world." It may be nice for this employee and others to imagine Harley as this indestructible behemoth, unsullied by bad practice, but it isn't true.

Cultural Mythmaking at Alberto-Culver

A similar situation arose at Alberto-Culver, where opinions about the origins of the company's culture differed dramatically between long-term employees and newer hires. Those who had been around for a long time usually remembered the former Alberto-Culver for its harsh, results-oriented, and isolating culture, but one member of the guiding coalition had a more nostalgic view that put Leonard Lavin in the role of the mythological father/creator and Alberto-Culver as this customer-focused master:

> Leonard Lavin had a good career doing a few things with business. He's out in California . . . and he ran across VO5 Hair Cream, which was a product that the actors and actresses were using to protect them under the klieg lights. So he thought it was a great product, he bought the company, he dropped every other product they made. He set up manufacturing here. . . . Started with a very small group of people, a very small business. Made a bunch of product. Put it in the trunk of his car and drove all over the country for a year selling it. Because, at that time, there were no chains, if you think about it, they were all independent stores. . . . They built up the business, and as you know from our financial performance we've continued to grow. And that's because there has been attention to what the consumer wants. . . . I don't think that's been a deficiency. I think if anything the deficiency was not looking inward enough at the processes up until the nineties. We always were about the customer.

The idea that Alberto-Culver was "always about the customer" contradicts the recollections of most people involved with the company during its more difficult years. Yet the tendency to mythologize continued; newer hires repeated mythologizing stories about Leonard Lavin and Carol Bernick and attributed the company's collaborative culture to a sense of nostalgia and family ownership.

One newer hire exemplified this tendency when he told Gary about the Alberto-Culver practice of employee recognition. "They still give away the gifts!" he said. "My prior company, you get this crappy postcard in the mail for your anniversary. 'Here's your service pin. Here's your watch.' I got a twenty-year watch from [an employer]—it was in the mail! Here, they have you come up. You take a picture with Mr. Lavin, as the chairman, you know. It's that personal touch. . . . People don't do that anymore out in the real world. This is part of the hidden culture—the deeply rooted culture that hasn't gotten tainted yet!"

Another newer executive at Alberto-Culver had a less nostalgic view of the company's success. Nonetheless, he downplayed the contribution of the company as a whole and largely attributed change to the sales function and the new sales executive, Dick Hynes, who was one of the last executives hired by Bernick later in her tenure.

"Six to nine months after Dick Hynes got here is when our top line started *roaring,*" he said. "When Dick got here, he was doing all the right stuff. He was bringing in all the right people. . . . Marketing efforts can only take you so far. In the consumer products industry you *need* to have a sales organization that's putting the . . . efforts on top of the marketing efforts. You know, promotional efforts that the sales guys and the customer marketing guys think of. That can swing a business. . . . We could still be treading water with the old sales organization."

Technophilia at Marshfield DoorSystems

An even stranger phenomenon arose at Marshfield DoorSystems, where newer hires credited a new enterprise resource planning (ERP) system for the company's improved ability to deliver to customer specifications. Anyone who has lived through an ERP implementation knows that crediting a piece of software for positive organizational behavior change is a misattribution. A major

ERP implementation is far more likely to calcify dysfunction into firm processes than it is to encourage change.

A more accurate reading of what happened at Marshfield is that the value proposition and formal work to establish a Shared Market Understanding happened first. Once that work was in place, the company realized that it needed some technological upgrades to support the operational changes it had undergone. The firm implemented DoorBuilder, as the ERP solution was called, in response to those needs, but the cultural and process changes responsible for the company turnaround were already producing significant results. Unfortunately, newcomers who came on board after the bulk of change took place were not aware of the sequence of events. Their primary source of reference was two widely read articles on Marshfield DoorSystems that had been published in *Businessweek* and the *Wall Street Journal* giving DoorBuilder top billing.[1]

SUCCESSFUL APPROACHES TO MAINTAINING CHANGE

The tendency within so many companies to create stories that allow them to see their market-focused culture as innate or somehow unchangeable has the potential to pose a real danger to the firm's ability to maintain its market focus. Those attitudes about the inherent nature of the culture remove agency from the individual. The collaborative investment that went into change dissipates. The focus and feel for the market are no longer something that everyone agrees to work on and commit to. They think it just happens on its own because the company *is*. If that perspective becomes too pervasive, then the ongoing commitment to the market erodes. To avoid this erosion, companies work to maintain the turnaround through a number of focused actions that reinforce and reemphasize the company's raison d'être.

Though each company follows a different path, we have identified five approaches that market-focused companies use to maintain that culture and perspective.

Screening New Hires

Companies that are successful at maintaining change are all very selective about who they bring into the company.

Alberto-Culver established a set of heuristics around the qualities of collaboration, communication, and teamwork, and used that structure to screen potential hires during the recruitment process. Management candidates that made it further through the process had to be approved by Carol Bernick before being given an offer, and she was directly involved in all executive hires. In this way she kept tight control of the culture by carefully selecting those with the most power within the organization.

One informant said of the process used to screen new hires at Alberto-Culver, "I think we've improved what we look for . . . in new employees and I think we're successfully raising the bar for the people here in the building. . . . Part of the turnover perhaps that we had in the past was we didn't have the kind of people that are fired up the way I hope most people are today, to make this place a winning place. That helps the buy-in and then that feeds into more success."

Marshfield DoorSystems was similar to Alberto-Culver in its use of heuristics to discern whether recruits were a good fit. Company executives made almost every hiring decision and relied heavily on referrals from existing employees.

Diligence on the part of leadership was critical to make that screening process work. That diligence was disrupted at Marshfield DoorSystems because Weyerhaeuser had sold the company to a private equity firm. The new owners installed a new CEO

(Bill Blankenship stayed with Weyerhaeuser; Jerry Mannigel stayed with Marshfield as president), who then hired a number of additional executives. The private equity firm had little basis to determine cultural alignment, with the predictable result that the behavior of the new executives was not consistent with the communicative, collaborative culture that Marshfield had worked so hard to create under Blankenship and Mannigel. This disruption created some temporary fissures in the Marshfield DoorSystems market-focused foundations. But as we described in the previous chapter on passing power to the employees, there were people who'd remained at Marshfield DoorSystems and who had lived through the change process. They had already taken over responsibility for asserting the culture. It was remarkable to see, in fact, how the new executives were called to task by hourly workers for not maintaining communication and sharing all the critical information from the market that they—the workers—needed to do their jobs.

When it came to screening new hires for their cultural fit, Harley-Davidson needed a more formal system than the one Marshfield DoorSystems used, one that was less dependent on the review of the executive team. Harley-Davidson had eight thousand employees, after all, and was growing dramatically once its turnaround was complete. There was no possibility that its senior executives could review every hire.

Instead, the company created some clear recruiting methods to ensure that its culture was maintained throughout the workforce. One executive who joined Harley before the LBO explained the training process that she and other leaders with the company had gone through to learn how to effectively interview a candidate and look for the kind of skills and cultural behaviors that the company needed. She said, "There are twenty different things/characteristics we look for. We still use this today. Some of the skills are: coping mechanisms, communications, energizing/the ability to energize, policy and procedures for people who work the line who you want to follow certain procedures, alertness, analytical problem solving, ability to set goals, written communication, creativity, decision making, et cetera. There might be five things I probe for a project manager, but probe for five completely different things for a [member of the same team]. Also I look for how do you work with those people over the long haul? How do you develop your staff?"

The cultural screening process that Harley-Davidson adopted resulted in a workforce whose individual members shared a number of common denominators. In Gary's interactions with them, Harley employees were uniformly trusting, open, honest, respectful, empathetic, dependable, and collaborative, and had an intense interest and concern for customers and dealers. This uniformity in values and behaviors held despite the striking individuality of the employees.

The core characteristics of Harley-ness appeared instrumental to the ongoing success of the firm, and the company took pains to ensure that the right types of people were invited to join. One informant said, "When you bring people into the organization that don't understand the tradition, your product suffers terribly. The neat thing about Harley-Davidson is we've managed to keep people coming in who understand the tradition. So the culture at the Motor Company absorbs them because they're ready to be absorbed and there's no conflict."

Cultural Onboarding and Refreshers

Once they have the right people on board, companies see the need to indoctrinate these employees with the right training and preparation. We talked about this a little bit in the previous chapter when we mentioned some of the systems that companies put in place to formalize change.

Harley-Davidson, for instance, began offering formal training programs to indoctrinate new hires and offer existing employees a periodic refresher on the culture and goals of the firm. One employee who joined the firm in 1990 recalled, "When I came here there was an awful lot of formal training. . . . Within a few months of me being here we had a new employee orientation. It was like the first one they had had. It lasted a half a day. And it was everybody who had started over the last six months. Now they do it, it starts every week and it lasts three days. But it was a smaller company then. . . ."

The same informant recalled receiving a copy of Peter Reid's 1990 book, *Well Made in America: Lessons from Harley-Davidson on Being the Best*, which tells the story of Harley-Davidson's transformation during the 1980s. "I read that one too before I started. They gave it to you before you started. Or at least they gave it to me."

Tenured employees were given similar cultural refresher courses in the form of the Leadership Institute program that was established in the 1990s. The Leadership Institute program involved six nonconsecutive weeks of training. The program combined classroom teaching, case analysis, practice exercises, and experiential training similar to Outward Bound. Not all these methods were embraced without reservation by the employees, however. In particular, the Outward Bound exercises were met with a great deal of nervousness and even resistance. Curiously, that resistance was grounded in a belief that the Outward Bound activities actually moved Harley away from its culture of genuine, honest interaction. The manufactured nature of trust activities rubbed a number of people the wrong way.

The classroom sessions, however, were widely appreciated. One informant said, "It was a great way of kind of just putting things on the table and having people discuss them. There's always the stuff which is valuable at different levels, which is how you manage people and things like that. Now, what I think was more valuable was when [we] went into the phase of understanding us as a company and our values and our vision and our business process model and understanding what that was. . . . And I think that that is probably more valuable today; to allow people to interact and understand events and come to some philosophy that was practical for them. It takes that philosophy and makes it practical for them. 'What does "tell the truth" mean to you? What does the vision statement [mean to you]? What are stakeholders? A shareholder is a stakeholder—no more, no less than some of these other stakeholders.' To really get those issues out on the table and have the discussions about them."

One executive commenting on the importance of these efforts said, "They really taught employees a lot about themselves in relation to their culture and how to reinforce themselves within the culture and therefore be more successful in the marketplace. That was the theme throughout the *whole thing*. And Teerlink actually said this—it's almost a direct quote—is that 'The danger is not in the competition. The danger is from within if we don't stick together; understand ourselves and our products; and understand how to work with one another effectively. Leverage the product and make it what the customer wants.'"

Alberto-Culver relied less on formal training to indoctrinate new hires and maintain cultural standards with veterans and more on the established GDL program and on other formal processes for communication.

As one approach, Bernick and her team put strong emphasis on the use of those Individual Economic Value Statements that the GDLs were tasked with creating for each employee. One Alberto-Culver manager described the importance of IEVs for helping people recognize their contribution to the business and be reminded, over time, of why they were all here. "Now, for instance, [in my area, for the line people, most of] theirs are very similar. They're probably all the same. But they know why they're here. If you don't know why you're here, how do you know that you're making a difference? That's a real important thing to get that into people's hands that understand it. Everyone in the building should drive sales and profits."

Alberto-Culver further enforced the importance of IEVs by including them as part of the evaluation process for GDLs. One informant said, "One of the awards in the GDL thing is the IEV award. If you're filling out the survey, you better have IEVs, they better be on your badge and they better mean something to you. They better really explain what your lot in life is. If you answer that question positively on behalf of your GDL, your GDL gets the IEV award for making sure that you have it, that you wear it and that they're meaningful to you. But if someone doesn't get called up for that award . . ."

Getting those top marks was important to any manager or executive at Alberto-Culver who wanted to advance. It was not enough to perform in their function. An employee could get top functional marks, but if he or she was a GDL as well, and if his or her performance ratings in that realm were average or below average, that employee was not going to advance.

Carol Bernick wrote about the program and the annual feedback process that "we sit down and talk with all the GDLs about their results and what's behind them. I personally pore over these surveys. I fret over the people who've shown a downturn; I marvel at those who've outdone themselves. Right now, I'm thinking about the conversation I'll have with one recent hire. She's great at what she does and very much in demand by team leaders around the company, but her GDL scores aren't impressive. My take is, she has the ability but hasn't realized how seriously we take this. Next year, I'd lay money on it, she'll be up toward the front of the pack."

In this way, Alberto-Culver used the GDL program not only to create a culture of communication and collaboration in the business, but also to assign new hires a cultural mentor and give established employees periodic refreshers or reminders.

In addition to leveraging the GDL program, Alberto-Culver leaders established a periodic meeting with brand teams a few times a year to give them open access to leadership and provide help and feedback. The meeting was named internally "Show and Sell." One participant explained, "The brand teams get top management in a substantial conference room and we also get a bunch of other people from other functions, and we present all the *stuff*—the cool *stuff*—that we're working on. . . . Here's the stuff that's starting to percolate up, that's in different stages of development. Some things may be just pure ideas, some things may have gone through qualitative testing, some things may have been validated and kinda ready to be pushed through, some things may be quantitatively tested and they failed. But we have that discussion about that mass of ideas and initiatives.

"From that, we sift and evolve. There's an example of how I think we're doing interaction with management in a very positive way. Because it's not like one of those classic Procter [& Gamble] meetings where you bring your book and you have to know every fact. It's not a test. It's an open discussion. And it's direct. . . . It gets our younger people excited about their ability to demonstrate some thinking, and get closer to management. . . . Was it in place when I first got here? No. Absolutely not. And it's something I never did at other companies. If I ever go to some other place, I would *absolutely* think that this would be a tool that could be beneficial."

The combined use of GDLs and direct leadership contact with frontline managers works for Alberto-Culver, but there is no one way to introduce a new employee to the company and their job. Companies that crafted stories or captured videos of field visits have concrete artifacts that they can use to introduce new employees to the Shared Market Understanding held within the organization or to share insights and important ideas with people in a dynamic way.

Ongoing Market Connections

Continually connecting with the market is another important means for maintaining a market orientation. Market-focused companies did other types of market research, such as focus groups and surveys. But as we noted in Chapter 7, it is difficult to accurately interpret market data without up-to-date observational experiences from the field. The companies that successfully maintain their market focus formalize periodic visits out to the field for one-on-one interactions with customers in the contexts in which they use the product. These visits allowed the team members themselves to see how the market might have shifted or needs adjusted, and those stories and insights were brought back to the company and shared through meetings and presentations, so that the Shared Market Understanding was consistently maintained or updated for everyone.

One senior marketing executive at Alberto-Culver said of the practice, "We do workshops around it—and I'll sit through some too—of the stuff in the field. . . . As much experience as I have in this category, it continues to change and people's beliefs change. So you have to stay with it and understand it. Because sometimes my experience can be detrimental—I have a lot more baggage than most. I have to understand when something's outdated and when things change. So I try to get out there as often as I can."

Alberto-Culver complemented field visits with other sources of measurable feedback on how the company is delivering value to the customer. Another executive explained, "Some of the other things we do is surveys and benchmarks particularly on the logistics side, which is essentially customer fulfillment, we benchmark ourselves against other companies—competitors—in this category. And it talks about a number of dimensions—customer service, costs, delivery times, cycle times. . . . What we do is we're very visible in terms of our service metrics. So everybody in the organization knows what our case fill is, what our service is—we make that very public. And we have targets that we have to hit that we feel are appropriate."

That same executive also refers to the daily meetings, discussed in a previous chapter, that take place between customer service and manufacturing. This meeting serves as a consistent check on how the company is serving the market. "Basically, if there's problems, everybody hears about it every day. So it's almost instantaneous feedback. . . . I'm a real believer in every day sitting down and kind of assessing what's going on with the business. That keeps the whole organization connected to where the issues are so that we can react together."

Marshfield DoorSystems likewise took steps to continually collect customer insights. Based on the work Marshfield did to define and validate its value proposition, it engaged an outside vendor to conduct semiannual, anonymous surveys of market players (channels, influencers, etc.) to test the ongoing validity of that value proposition and to monitor changes. This work allowed Marshfield to gauge its success at delivering to the value proposition. At the same time, it got a fairly objective sense of how its offerings compared with others'.

Marshfield did not stop there. Beyond the survey work, it also continued to do field visits, particularly to test or assess the market for new products or changes. For example, in early 2002, the company saw that it needed to update the value proposition for its composites division; before it did that, it sent cross-functional teams into the field to interview buyers to document what those constituents valued and how that had changed.

Harley-Davidson had the greatest opportunity to make ongoing market connections through continued use of the demo rides and the HOG rides, which it had set up in the early years of its transformation. As at the beginning of its transformation, these personal connections not only serve as a way to gather data about the experience of the customer; they also energize and engage the employee.

As one twenty-plus-year veteran of the firm commented, "Even when I go to rallies now . . . I come back with a greater sense of contribution to the business, visioning, and focus than I had before. I'm hearing our needs, but it's good to get those needs either validated or repositioned hearing it from the customer. . . . I don't have to go to demo rides anymore but I just wanted to. . . . Every opportunity you get to leave these four walls you always learn something. I also go to a dealer almost every other month. It impacts how I direct resources, how I get projects approved, how I run projects—everything."

Many companies give their employees special access to company products or services in the form of internal company stores or special discounts available at retail locations. Harley-Davidson operates differently. The company program that encourages employees to buy Harley-Davidson motorcycles requires that they purchase and service their personal bikes through dealerships, just as any customer would. There is no employee fleet. One informant explained, "You have to go to a dealer, you have to get in line with everybody else. You've got to order a bike . . . you make the best deal you can get. So the employees, in order to use the product, have to have the customer experience. We're not insulated behind a privileged fleet of bikes."

To that point, during Gary's fieldwork he met a number of Harley-Davidson employees who worked for years on development and production of the V-Rod and still had not managed to buy one because there were waiting lists at the dealerships!

Cultural Flame Keepers

As firms moved further away from the intense early days of change, and as they continued to adjust to market needs, they were inevitably faced with making strategic or procedural choices that affected the culture of the firm. It is not always obvious how to balance the conflicting demands of the market with other stake-holders—owners, employees, traditional customers versus future or evolving customers, etc.

The companies that successfully maintained change had cultural flame keepers whose implicit or explicit role was to ensure that procedures or programs adopted in the effort to further improve the organization did not cut against the organization's market-oriented culture.

For example, a number of Marshfield DoorSystems executives visited another firm and heard about an employee program that required people to make improvement suggestions. If an idea was chosen and implemented, the employee who suggested it got a bonus. A number of executives liked the idea and thought it should be put in place at Marshfield. But a Marshfield executive who was part of the change coalition asked if such a program was inconsistent with the Marshfield DoorSystems culture. Employee suggestion boxes could encourage team members to keep their good ideas for the suggestion box, rather than sharing them with their peers in an everyday mode of collaboration and problem solving.

The coalition executive summarized his concern: "[That] firm culture won't work here at Marshfield where there is a culture of trust—where you treat people like adults." He then observed the problem with creating extrinsic incentives that allow people to game the system, instead of the current focus on improving the overall operations for the sake of everyone: "So if a suggestion is *not* hiring two summer [interns] does that count? It saves money. It's not the right thing to do by any means, but it saves money. Does that count? How are we going to do this right? It can't count."

In the end, the executive team decided the idea went against the way Marshfield did things and the program was not implemented.

Marshfield's approach to cultural flame keeping was in many ways democratic, with the responsibility held by everyone, especially past coalition members. Cultural flame keeping at Alberto-Culver also relied on past coalition members for its stability. Carol Bernick was the lead flame keeper, as demonstrated by the ongoing interest and investment she put into reviewing GDL performance and monitoring the progress of various members. Bernick also kept her Workplace 2000 coalition intact, but she renamed it and adjusted its membership to give different people opportunities to contribute to cultural maintenance.

Alberto-Culver continued to invest in rewarding and acknowledging people for their contributions—sometimes in the face of resistance. One coalition member said, "Up until last year, we had all the GDLs, every quarter, nominate the above-and-beyond awards. . . . And we got to the point that the GDLs would say, 'Again? I gotta do it again?' Yeah you do. We're forcing you to do it. Because you know what? In a fast-paced environment, the first thing you forget about is your people. It always is. Because you've got deadlines, you've tangible things you've got to do. And doing the little things like recognizing people and thanking them is really the first thing that typical people forget. But Carol pushes all that and sincerely pushes it. And people across the company know that's our culture. And they give back. So I think it's a true relationship between the company and the employees."

Resisting Fads

Technology change, market adjustments, economic shifts, and dozens of other factors can introduce management trends that have such momentum and power in the market that they are difficult to resist. Some of these trends may have staying power and can be good additions within a market-oriented culture. Others are inconsistent with the approach adopted by the business. It is not always easy to know which you are dealing with; companies that successfully maintain their core market orientation despite fad temptations seem able to take a step back and ask, "Is this consistent with our culture? Does it help us do our work better?"

Harley-Davidson found itself asking these questions in the 2000s when it was being encouraged to invest in a customer relationship management (CRM) software system. ("CRM" is a catchall term that encompasses front-office activity and processes around sales, marketing, and customer service.)

Harley-Davidson's dealers have a lot of data about their customers, and Harley-Davidson corporate likewise maintains its own databases. Those systems don't talk to each other. For some it is a no-brainer that Harley would want to know and use all the data it could about the customer, but when Gary spoke to informants at the company they communicated thoughtful resistance to the idea that having and using data were consistent with what Harley-Davidson is. One informant questioned whether the fad was right for Harley out of a concern for seeming intrusive. "I hear people say, 'The real power of Harley-Davidson is the power to market to consumers who love the product.' . . . If it's true, should we change that? Why would we get closer? Why would we appear intrusive?"

Harley-Davidson had not yet decided whether to implement a CRM system or what it would look like. The point is that market-focused companies must be wary of—but in many ways are in a position to resist—fads that might threaten how the company has positioned itself. Like Harley-Davidson, they are able to consider new trends and reflect on their appropriateness by viewing them through the lens of what the company is and what the market values from it.

As one Harley-Davidson executive said, "My big focus has always been to know who you are and who you're not. And be consistent, because it is just painful to watch certain brands who have tried so many different positionings. Or have tried to 'freshen' their brand. And they end up being something that they weren't. My belief is that the brand identity model should very, very rarely change. It has tweaks, but it doesn't change."

CONCLUSION

Companies that have progressed to the point where they can maintain change often see how stories or myths are developed to explain the changes that took place and the company that has come about to this day. These myths are dangerous when they replace a collective and cooperative set of actions with a view of change that credits one heroic figure, or some historical legacy that the company possesses irrespective of the people who lead it.

Maintenance requires moving against the tendency to back-slide by embracing a set of practices that keep the market-focused culture alive within the firm. Companies that successfully maintain change actively:

- Screen new hires for cultural behaviors that are consistent with the culture of the business.
- Run detailed training and cultural orientation for new hires.
- Offer refresher programs for veteran companies.
- Maintain ongoing connection with the customer.
- Appoint cultural flame keepers.
- Avoid fads and fashions.

From this strong foundation, successfully resurgent firms are equipped to reap the benefits of change for the long term.

CONCLUSION

13

REAPING THE BENEFITS OF CHANGE

MUCH HAS CHANGED SINCE 1981, WHEN HARLEY-Davidson's new team of owners launched their effort to reinvent the failing motorcycle manufacturer. With less than 5 percent US motorcycle market share, the Harley leaders knew the very survival of the company was at stake. They turned to the remaining employees and to the union to build a culture of collaboration, honesty, and trust within the organization. And then they turned to the market to understand fundamentally what the customer wanted and expected from the company. With that foundation in place, Harley-Davidson again started to grow.

By 2003, when Harley-Davidson celebrated its centenary, the company was almost unrecognizable compared to the stagnant, complacent one it had been twenty years before. Gone was the reputation for poor quality and slow change. From single-digit market share, Harley-Davidson had risen from its decline to deliver a more reliable, higher-quality product, designed with the customer in mind and built in a collaborative environment. The market liked the new Harley-Davidson and customers responded with their wallets.

There is no clearer testament to the success of change than growth. From near obsolescence, Harley-Davidson came to recapture more than 50 percent of the US heavyweight-motorcycle market. The company went public in 1986, and from that year to 2003 it earned 37 percent annual growth in its stock price.[1] At the height of sales in 2006, before the global financial crisis decimated all sectors of the automotive market, Harley-Davidson earned a record profit of more than $1 billion. Despite the beating it took with the economic downturn, Harley-Davidson was holding fast to 65 percent of the US motorcycle market, far ahead of the 13 percent share held by second-place Honda.[2]

Harley-Davidson had certainly known success before. But even in the 1950s when it was one of the only surviving motorcycle companies in the United States, it was in no way the celebrated, embraced icon it is today. The legendary rider culture that so many associate with the essence of Harley did not exist before the demo rides and HOG rides that were instituted as part of its effort to become more market-focused. Harley's very identity today rests on the fact that its leadership in the early 1980s had the courage to see that change was needed, and the humility to recognize that change would need to be guided by the market.

By no means is the changed Harley-Davidson immune to competitive pressures. The global financial crisis that began in 2007 brought significant declines in sales and profits, but even before that the company was facing criticism from Wall Street for its aging core audience and a segmented motorcycle market. It has been a long time since Harley-Davidson was a media and analyst darling. As the market leader, Harley-Davidson receives particular scrutiny, criticized for the way its loyalty to legacy and tradition puts it at risk as its core rider population—white male baby boomers—are aging out of the market.

Yet look closer. Change is inevitable. At any given time a new competitor, new technology, or shift in the market can challenge an established position. But Harley-Davidson is no stranger to change. Its leaders realized more than thirty years ago that in order to survive the company needed stronger in-house communication and collaboration and tighter connections to its market. As a result of that hard work and effort, the Harley-Davidson that competes today is a far stronger and more profitable company than it ever was in the past. One thousand dollars invested in Harley-Davidson after it went public has grown to $14,000 in 2012, beating the S&P 500 seventeen times over. In 2012 more than half of all Harley-Davidson motorcycle unit sales were purchased by customers new to the company and buying their first Harley-Davidson. The company saw particular growth with women, minorities, and young people under the age of thirty-five—not the traditional Harley-Davidson rider. The company did not realize change just to survive. It realized change, continued to change, and achieved far greater success than it had ever achieved in the past.

CHANGE BRINGS GREATER SUCCESS THAN BEFORE

Harley-Davidson's experience is not unique. A number of firms we observed realized a market-focused resurgence to become not just competitive again, but stronger than they ever had been.

Consider Alberto-Culver: it had been a mid-market provider focusing on skin and hair care, a respected, respectable company, but never a market leader in the categories in which it competed. The change effort initiated by Carol Bernick and her Workplace 2000 coalition completely changed the organization. It went from being entirely dependent upon the entrepreneurial imagination of Leonard Lavin to reinventing itself as an innovator of new lines and products. It went from being known largely as the manufacturer of the Alberto VO5 line of hair care products, to a multibrand company known for innovating in product development and market strategy and for making focused, strategic decisions, such as the 2007 divestment of the Sally Beauty Supply business.

In 2009, a difficult year for pretty much every market, Alberto-Culver's TRESemmé brand of hair care products was the fastest-growing hair care brand and the leading hair-styling brand in the country. The product development team was coming up with new ideas for TRESemmé customers, such as a new "dry" shampoo for a growing market segment. Worldwide, TRESemmé is also strong in markets such as the United Kingdom, Spain, and South Africa, and had just launched in Portugal. Likewise Nexxus, a known and respected salon-quality brand, grew faster than other brands in that portion of the market to reach double-digit growth. And Alberto VO5 held its place as a relevant entry-level product and as the leading styling brand in the United Kingdom.[3]

These achievements attracted attention: in 2011 Unilever agreed to buy Alberto-Culver for $3.7 billion in cash, more than two and a half times Alberto-Culver's fiscal year 2010 earnings.

Marshfield DoorSystems likewise saw greater success after its change efforts than it had ever experienced before. When Jerry Mannigel and Bill Blankenship initiated the change effort in the mid-1990s, the company was losing millions on around $50 million in revenue. By the time Gary was embedded at Marshfield doing the field research, the company had already rebounded to the point that it had 2001 sales of $120 million and 2001 profit of $10 million. More recently, Marshfield DoorSystems has developed a number of innovations and enjoyed strong growth in developing countries, which offset some of the challenges it faced as of 2007 in slower-growth developed markets. These changes made Marshfield very attractive, even in a time of stagnation in construction and building industries. In 2011, WindPoint Partners, the private equity firm that had owned Marshfield since 2001, sold the company to Masonite International, one of the largest door manufacturers in the world, with 2012 revenues of more than $1.6 billion. Masonite purchased Marshfield Door-Systems for $102.4 million, $45.6 million more than the fair market value of its assets.[4]

FAILING TO FORMALIZE CHANGE

The news for Motorola and its PCS division is more mixed. The change effort spearheaded by Mike Zafirovski and blessed by Chris Galvin had achieved significant changes within the PCS division by around 2003. The employees there were working together. They were more respectful of the contributions that non-engineering personnel could make to product development, and more aware and considerate of the ways in which the end-user customer utilized the phone. These changes resulted in the creation of the RAZR, a huge product success that in the mid-2000s temporarily stopped the downward slide of Motorola's mobile handset market share.

That success was, sadly, temporary. When Gary was embedded doing research at Motorola, the company had reconnected with the customer to create a Shared Market Understanding, and it was using that Shared Understanding to develop effective market and product development strategy. In 2003 a product development team was working on the highly successful RAZR, the clamshell-style mobile phone that was the PCS jewel in the crown for four years and sold more than 130 million units worldwide between 2004 and 2008.[5] But change was still vulnerable in that phase, and Motorola had not yet done much to formalize those changes. For that reason and others, change did not hold.

It began to lose hold of its change efforts significantly beginning in 2003, when Motorola experienced another round of leadership upheaval, beginning with the departure of Chris Galvin, who stepped down due to board pressure. Mike Zafirovski, the president and COO at the time and heir apparent to Galvin's seat, was passed over for the top spot and resigned from his number-two position. That disruption was further exacerbated by the sudden and tragic death in 2005 of Motorola's dynamic CMO, Geoffrey Frost, a staunch advocate for the market perspective.

Collectively, the loss of these change leaders, coupled with the vulnerable status of Motorola's change effort, badly crippled the company. Motorola relied on the success of the RAZR and missed or ignored the market switch to smartphones. When Apple's iPhone launched in the summer of 2007, Motorola didn't have a relevant product to compete in the category. By 2006 Motorola had sold 50 million RAZR handsets; by 2008 those sales had slowed to a trickle, leading to Motorola's spinoff of the PCS division as Motorola Mobility, which was purchased in 2012 for $12.5 billion by Google.

The stories of change for both the once-independent Alberto-Culver and Motorola end with acquisition, but the companies are similar only in the abstract. Alberto-Culver was bought for its strong consumer beauty brands by a company looking to grow in that segment; Motorola, in contrast, was bought because it was weak. Unable to formalize change, it slipped, lost touch, and went back to building products that no one wanted and that couldn't compete in the explosive era of the iPhone.

MARKET FOCUS: A RECIPE FOR SUCCESS

Throughout this book we have made the case that stagnating companies—businesses that have lost the momentum of growth—

can reinvent themselves through market-focused change. We told the stories of seven companies that worked to breathe new life into their operations. Four of them managed through dedicated, multiyear efforts to return to success, if only temporarily. Three never progressed far past the point of recognizing the need for change.

This is not the story of just seven companies, however. It is the story of hundreds of businesses that grow for a time and then begin to decline, challenged by a change in technology or infrastructure, by new competitive demands or market dynamics. This story is about Alberto-Culver, Harley-Davidson, Marshfield DoorSystems, Motorola, BenefitsInc, EquipmentCo, and MediaCo, as much as it is about Avon and JCPenney, McDonald's and Starbucks, eBay, and dozens of others. All these businesses have seen that they were ill prepared to adapt to fundamental change. But change is essential for survival.

The difference between those businesses that have been successful—realizing a sustained resurgence—and those that have not lies in the subtleties of managing change. In resurgent firms, willing and patient leaders recognize the need for a structured, multiyear path of change. Resurgent firms start from within, creating a vision for change, and work to transform the culture throughout the organization. Resurgent firms reach out to understand how customers think and feel; to understand expectations; to understand the challenges or hopes the customer has and how the business can best address them. Resurgent firms engage multiple functions in planning and developing products and strategies for the market. Resurgent firms make difficult decisions about who to keep, who to let go, and who to hire in order to build not just in-house skills but in-house culture and behaviors.

Finally, resurgent firms are persistent. They do not put in the hard work and effort of reinvention to then stop and let everything revert to its original form. Instead, they formalize and maintain change and then continue to adapt. They identify the compensation systems and organizational structures that are consistent with a trusting, open, collaborative environment built on reliability, accountability, and market focus. They put in place the recruiting and training processes needed to maintain a market-focused culture. And they keep connecting with the market. Repeatedly and consistently, they reach out to refresh their understanding of what the market wants and what they are in a position to provide.

There are no shortcuts to becoming market-focused. The change takes time, effort, and commitment. But the benefits are worth it. The gains are not just financial. They are also personal. Resurgent companies offer environments where people want to work every day. They are communities—inspiring places to work, where individuals see their role in achieving something substantial and good. But such organizations aren't born—they are made. Fortunately, making one starts with little more than recognition.

NOTES

CHAPTER 1

1. Both IBM and McKinsey have published recent research studies in which they each asked more than one thousand executives their views on recent change efforts within their businesses. In both studies, the average success rate was around 30 percent, meaning that 70 percent of change initiatives failed to meet their stated objectives. The IBM study furthermore showed that less-experienced change managers had only an 8 percent success rate. For more information, see: "Making Change Work," IBM Institute for Business Value, http://www-935.ibm.com/services/us/gbs/bus/html/gbs-making-change -work.html, accessed June 17, 2013; and McKinsey & Company, "The In-convenient Truth about Change Management," http://www.mckinsey.com /App_Media/Reports/Financial_Services/The_Inconvenient_Truth_About _Change_Management.pdf, accessed June 17, 2013.

2. Peter Drucker, *The Practice of Management* (New York: Harper & Row, 1954).

3. For more details, see Kohli and Jaworski's original paper: "Market Orientation: The Construct, Research Propositions, and Managerial Implications," *Journal of Marketing* 54 (April 1990): 1–18.

4. C. R. Cano, F. A. Carrillat, and F. Jaramillo, "A Meta-Analysis of the Relationship between Market Orientation and Business Performance: Evidence from Five Continents," *International Journal of Research in Marketing* 21, no. 2 (2004): 179–200; R. Deshpandé and J. U. Farley, "The Market Orientation Construct: Correlations, Culture, and Comprehensiveness," *Journal of Market-Focused Management* 2 (1998b): 237–39; A. H. Kirca, S. Jayachandran, and W. O. Bearden, "Market Orientation: A Meta-Analytic Review and Assessment of Its Antecedents and Impact on Performance," *Journal of Marketing* 69, no. 2 (2005): 24–41; and V. Kumar et al., "Is Market Orientation a Source of Sustainable Competitive Advantage or Simply the Cost of Competing?," *Journal of Marketing* 75, no. 1 (2011): 16–30.

5. Throughout the book, all quotes attributed to Carol Bernick, unless otherwise cited, were drawn from Carol Lavin Bernick, "When Your Culture Needs a Makeover," *Harvard Business Review* (June 2001).

CHAPTER 2

1. For more details on Harley-Davidson's history, see Suresh Kotha and John Dutton, "Transformation at Harley-Davidson," Stern School of Business, New York University (1996).

2. Market share numbers from Kotha and Dutton, "Transformation at Harley-Davidson."
3. Details on the history of Alberto-Culver supplemented from in-person interviews with details from the following article: Judith Crown, "Split Decision," *Chicago Magazine* (May 2006), http://www.chicagomag.com/Chicago-Magazine/May-2006/Split-Decision/, accessed June 11, 2013.
4. Unless otherwise noted, all direct quotes attributed to Carol Bernick come from Carol Lavin Bernick, "When Your Culture Needs a Makeover," *Harvard Business Review* (June 2001).

CHAPTER 4

1. Jim Collins and Jerry Porras, *Built to Last: Successful Habits of Innovative Companies* (New York: HarperBusiness, 2004).
2. John Kotter, "How to Create a Powerful Vision for Change," *Forbes.com*, June 7, 2011, http://www.forbes.com/sites/johnkotter/2011/06/07/how-to-create-a-powerful-vision-for-change/, accessed June 12, 2013.
3. Details from this case derived from Gregory Carpenter, *eBay Marketplace*, Kellogg School of Management, September 2011.
4. See Brad Stone, "In Sale, Skype Wins a Chance to Prosper," *New York Times*, September 1, 2009; and Peter Bright, "Microsoft Buys Skype for $8.5 Billion. Why, Exactly?" *Wired*, May 10, 2011.
5. Peter Burrows, "EBay Outlines Three-Year Revival Plan," *BusinessWeek*, March 12, 2009.

CHAPTER 5

1. Peter Reid, *Well Made in America, Lessons from Harley-Davidson on Being the Best* (New York: McGraw-Hill, 1990).
2. Howard Schultz, *Onward: How Starbucks Fought for Its Life Without Losing Its Soul* (New York: Rodale Books, 2011).
3. For more details on the events leading up to McDonald's change efforts, and the early steps it took to remake itself, see "Did Somebody Say a Loss?" *Economist*, April 10, 2003; and "McDonald's Hamburger Hell," *Bloomberg BusinessWeek*, March 2, 2003.

CHAPTER 6

1. Albert Bandura, *Social Learning Theory* (Englewood Cliffs, NJ: Prentice Hall, 1977).
2. Edgar Schein, *Organizational Culture and Leadership* (San Francisco: Jossey-Bass, 1985).
3. See Peter Reid, *Well Made in America: Lessons from Harley-Davidson on Being the Best* (New York: McGraw-Hill, 1990); and Richard Nolan and Suresh Kotha, "Harley-Davidson: Preparing for the Next Century," Cambridge: Harvard Business School, April 5, 2007, ed. 9-906-410.
4. For more details see: Samantha Pearson, "Avon: Not Feeling the Love in Brazil," *FT.com*, April 3, 2012, http://blogs.ft.com/beyond-brics/2012/04/03/avon-not-feeling-the-love-in-brazil/?#axzz2WCth0uhr, accessed June 14, 2013; and Beth Kowitt, "The Rise and Fall of a Beauty Icon," *Fortune*, April 11, 2012.

CHAPTER 8

1. When Ron Johnson took over as chief executive officer, he hired a group of executives to lead the turnaround with him. Among them were marketing chief Michael Francis, COO Michael Kramer, and chief talent officer Daniel Walker. They have all been dismissed with Johnson in the aftermath of the failed turnaround. See Matt Townsend, "J.C. Penney Spent $170 Million to Install Johnson Team," *Bloomberg.com*, May 3, 2013, http://www.bloomberg .com/news/2013-05-03/j-c-penney-spent-170-million-to-install-johnson -team.html, accessed May 28, 2013.
2. Susan Berfield, "Remaking JCPenney Without Coupons," *Bloomberg Businessweek*, May 24, 2012.
3. Jennifer Reingold, "Ron Johnson: Retail's New Radical," *CNNMoney*, March 7, 2012.
4. Sapna Maheshwari, "JCPenney's Lowest Sales in Decades Show Johnson's Stumbles," *Bloomberg Businessweek*, February 28, 2013.
5. Ibid.

CHAPTER 9

1. James B. Stewart, "Behind eBay's Comeback," *New York Times*, July 27, 2012.
2. Karen O'Leonard, *The Talent Acquisition Factbook 2011* (Bersin & Associates, November 2011). The data collected for this publication also showed that companies spend an average of $3,500 on recruitment per hire.

CHAPTER 10

1. Bernard Jaworski and Ajay Kohli, "Market Orientation: Antecedents and Consequences," *Journal of Marketing* 57, no. 3 (July 1993): 53–70.
2. Carol Lavin Bernick, "When Your Culture Needs a Makeover," *Harvard Business Review* (June 2001).
3. Richard Teerlink and Lee Ozley, *More Than a Motorcycle: The Leadership Journey at Harley-Davidson* (Cambridge: Harvard Business Press, 2000).
4. Ibid.
5. Ibid.
6. Ibid.
7. See Harley-Davidson's 1998 annual report: http://www.harley-davidson.com /company/investor/ar/1998/leadership/unions.asp.
8. Teerlink and Ozley, *More Than a Motorcycle*.

CHAPTER 12

1. Marcia Stepanek, "How an Intranet Opened Up the Door to Profits," *BusinessWeek*, July 25, 1999; and Bill Richards, "Making the Sale—A Total Overhaul," *Wall Street Journal*, December 7, 1998.

CHAPTER 13

1. Richard Nolan and Suresh Kotha, "Harley-Davidson: Preparing for the Next Century" (Cambridge: Harvard Business School, 2003).

2. Statistics from IBISWorld. See http://www.statista.com/statistics/252210
/market-share-of-major-motorcycle-manufacturers-in-the-us/, accessed June
13, 2013.

3. Alberto-Culver 2009 Annual Report.

4. Masonite International 2012 Annual Report: http://media.corporate-ir.net
/media_files/IROL/21/212381/financial/2012/Masonite-Q4-2011-Financial
-Update.pdf, accessed June 17, 2013.

5. Total Motorola RAZR units sold reported by the *Telegraph:* http://www
.telegraph.co.uk/technology/picture-galleries/9818080/The-20-bestselling
-mobile-phones-of-all-time.html?frame=2458999, accessed June 14, 2013.

ACKNOWLEDGMENTS

WE ARE INDEBTED TO MANY FOR THEIR SUPPORT IN COMPLETING THIS project. Foremost, we acknowledge and thank the executives, managers, and employees at the companies we studied, who welcomed us into their daily lives and shared their time, thoughts, and insights with us. We are deeply grateful to all of you for everything you shared with us. Our research and this book would not have possible without your openness and generosity.

We are grateful to our colleagues at the Northwestern's Kellogg School of Management who played a very important role helping shape our thinking about the work. In particular, Ed Zajac and Paul Hirsch of Kellogg's Management and Organizations department were instrumental in helping shape the methodological and conceptual aspects of the study. Our colleagues at Kellogg's Marketing Department, HEC Montreal, Notre Dame's Mendoza College of Business, University of South Florida, UCLA, Columbia, Emory and Harvard provided useful feedback on early versions of the work and significantly advanced our thinking and the quality of the book you have today.

Finishing this work was possible because of the support of many people. Dean Dipak Jain, interim Dean Sunil Chopra, and Dean Sally Blount of Northwestern University's Kellogg School of Management provided valuable support throughout the project that was essential to its completion. In addition to the support provided by the Kellogg School of Management, the Marketing Science Institute and the Institute for the Study of Business Markets provided significant financial support for which we are indebted.

Timothy Ogden and Laura Starita of Sona Partners are excellent editors and guides to transforming our research. We are grateful to Thomas C. Hayes for introducing us, for his encouragement, and for his guidance. Jacqueline Murphy of Inkwell Management was an early supporter and very effective advocate for which we are grateful. Karen Wolny and the team at Palgrave Macmillan have been have been enthusiastic since our first phone call and we're indebted for their support and their fine work bringing this project to fruition.

Finally, we would like to thank a number of specific individuals who helped make this research and its publication possible in various ways, including helping us identify and gain the cooperation of participating companies, offering comments and support before, during and after the research and publication process: Mike Barnett, Johanne Brunet, Stephen Burnett, François Carrillat, Anne Coughlin, Markus Giesler, Jeff Graves, Dominique Hanssens, Scott Hunter, Olin Hyde, Michael Jensen, Mark Kennedy, Ajay Kohli, Rob Kozinets, Tom Kuczmarksi, Renaud Legoux, Bill Locander, Deepak Malhotra, Jim McAlexander, John Narver, Jim

Oakley, Hayagreeva Rao, Ross Rizley, Roland Rust, Lou Sanchez, John Schouten, and James Ward.

Gregory S. Carpenter
James Farley/Booz Allen
Hamilton Professor of
Marketing Strategy
Director of the Center
for Market Leadership
Kellogg School
of Management,
Northwestern University

Gary F. Gebhardt
Associate Professor of
Marketing
HEC Montreal

John F. Sherry, Jr.
Herrick Professor &
Department Chair
Mendoza College /
Marketing & Professor
of Anthropology
(Concurrent)
University of Notre
Dame

ABOUT THE AUTHORS

GREGORY S. CARPENTER is the James Farley/Booz Allen Hamilton Professor of Marketing Strategy and director of the Center for Market Leadership at the Kellogg School of Management of Northwestern University, and he hosts the annual Kellogg Marketing Leadership Summit. He is a frequent speaker on marketing strategy and his research has been featured in *Harvard Business Review, Financial Times,* and on NPR.

GARY F. GEBHARDT is Associate Professor of Marketing at HEC Montreal. He teaches marketing strategy, market-focused innovation, B2B and channel marketing in the MBA, MSc, and McGill-HEC Montreal EMBA programs. He worked as a consultant and executive in industry for thirteen years before earning his PhD in Marketing at Northwestern's Kellogg School of Management.

JOHN F. SHERRY, JR. is Herrick Chair and Chairman of the Marketing Department at University of Notre Dame. An anthropologist, he taught at Northwestern's Kellogg School for over two decades. He has researched, lectured, and consulted around the globe on issues of brand strategy, experiential consumption, and retail atmospherics.

INDEX

customer focus, *See* market outreach
customer relationship management (CRM), 226

Davidson, Willie G., 73, 207–8
Daytona Bike Week, 116, 191–2, 195–7
demarcation events, 73–85
denial, 15–17, 21, 40
Deutsch, Adam, 83, 101
dissenters versus believers, 157–69
Donahoe, John, 26, 68–70, 166
Drucker, Peter, 7–8
Dunkin' Donuts, 76

Eagle Soars Alone ride (Harley-Davidson), 73–6, 78, 97
eBay, 11–12, 20, 27, 68–71, 166–7, 235
   and Buy It Now feature, 69
   and core customer, 68–71
   and market focus, 68–71
   and Bill Me Later, 70
   and warning signals, 20
   See John Donahoe
EMEA, *See* Europe, the Middle East, and Africa
employees, 11, 191–203, 214–21
   and culture, 193–5, 200–3
   and direct customer contact, 191–2
   and new hires, 214–21
   and power shifts, 192–3, 197–200
   and tools for power shifts, 197–200
   and vision, 193
   See collaborative strategy; layoffs; Shared Market Understanding
Ennis, Alan, 102
enterprise resource planning (ERP) system (Marshfield DoorSystems), 212–13
entrepreneurial organizations, 21, 51–2, 148
EquipmentCo, 9–10, 12, 19, 24, 33, 40–1, 60–2, 67, 81–4, 96, 100–2, 130, 149–50, 208, 235
   and coalition building, 33, 40–1
   and consulting firms, 60
   and demarcation events, 81–4
   and inconsistency, 100–2
   and leadership, 24
   and market focus, 130, 149–50
   and marketing, 67
   and messaging, 33
   and Reinvent, 9–10
   and training for change, 96
   and values, 60–2
ERB, *See* executive review board
ERP, *See* enterprise resource planning
ethnography, 10

Europe, the Middle East, and Africa (EMEA), 94
executive review board (ERB) (Motorola), 94–5, 121, 144–5

fad resistance, 11, 17, 226–7
Forbes, 1
Formalize stage (third stage), 4–5, 9, 11, 173–89, 191–203, 233, 235–6
   and compensation structures, 178–81
   and incentives, 173–6, 181–2
   and indoctrination, 186–8
   and making it official, 173–89
   and market focus, 177–86
   and employees, 11, 191–203
formula for market focus success, 135, 144, 155
four stages of reinvention
   See Formalize; Maintain; Recognize; Reinvent
Fuller, Buckminster, 207

Galvin, Chris, 23, 34, 57–8, 84–5, 233–4
   See Motorola
Galvin, Robert, 22
GDL, *See* Growth Development Leader
GE, 58–9, 85
Gebhardt, Gary F., 6, 10–12, 90, 100–1, 104, 123, 126, 135, 142–3, 145, 147, 166–7, 174, 188, 191–2, 195–7, 211–12, 216, 224, 226–7, 232–3
Gelb, Tom, 30, 96
Gerstner, Lou, 26
Godiva, 70–1
going public, *See* public commitment
Google, 234
Graves, Frank, 83
Great Depression, 18
Greenberg, Jack, 77
Growth Development Leader (GDL) (Alberto-Culver), 56, 80, 98, 125, 140, 173, 177, 180, 183, 186–7, 200–1, 218, 220–1, 225
GSI, 70

H&M, 150
Harley Owners Group (HOG), 93–4, 210, 223, 230
Harley-Davidson, 1, 3, 5–6, 9–10, 16–19, 22–3, 26, 29–30, 32–6, 38–9, 53, 59–60, 69, 73–81, 84–5, 92–7, 116–20, 123, 126, 130, 133–7, 148–50, 154, 160, 163–5, 171, 177–80, 182, 184–5, 191–2, 195–7, 205–10, 215–18, 223–4, 226–7, 229–31, 233–5
   and circle organization, 184–5